Figuratively Speaking

CLASSICAL INTER/FACES

Series editors: Susanna Braund and Paul Cartledge

FIGURATIVELY SPEAKING

Rhetoric and Culture from Quintilian to the Twin Towers

Sarah Spence

Duckworth

First published in 2007 by
Gerald Duckworth & Co. Ltd.
90-93 Cowcross Street, London EC1M 6BF
Tel: 020 7490 7300
Fax: 020 7490 0080
inquiries@duckworth-publishers.co.uk
www.ducknet.co.uk

A catalogue record for this book is available
from the British Library

ISBN 978 0 7156 3513 1

Typeset by e-type, Liverpool
Printed and bound in Great Britain by
CPI Bath

Contents

To Ned, who may well be a Jedi

Acknowledgments

The idea for this book was hatched many years ago and I have accrued many debts as a result. Thanks are owed to Susanna Braund and Paul Cartledge, series editors, and Deborah Blake, whose patience and commitment have been exemplary; to Philip Thibodeau, John Hollander and Eleanor Cook, who sharpened my notions of figures; to Keith Dix, Erika Hermanowicz, Donald Grathwohl, Leslie Harkema, Andrew Lemons, and Amanda Mathis, colleagues and graduate students at the University of Georgia who read and commented on chapter drafts; to my husband, Jim McGregor, who always knows what I mean to say; and to our son, the book's dedicatee, who has taught me much about the power and value of persuasion. Finally, deep gratitude is owed to Polly Chatfield, in whose beautiful apartment much of the first draft of this book was written as I listened to Bach and watched the river flow.

*

The section on Abbot Suger in Chapter 3 was adapted from 'What's Love Got to Do With It?', *Reading Medieval Culture: Essays in Honor of Robert W. Hanning*, ed. Robert Stein and Sandra P. Prior (Notre Dame, 2005), pp. 68-88. I have included the original text where the words themselves are under discussion; otherwise I have included only translations. All translations are my own unless otherwise indicated. In the Occitan texts quoted in Chapter 3, raised dots indicate enclitic contractions of the definite article, while apostrophes mark elision of the final vowel.

Introduction: Making Language Visible

'You don't want to sell me death sticks'.
'I don't want to sell you death sticks'.

'You want to go home and rethink your life'.
'I want to go home and rethink my life'.

Rhetoric is a Jedi mind trick. Like Obi-Wan Kenobi, the orator sets out to make you see things his way. If we were all Jedi, this book and the history of rhetoric it aims to illuminate would be very short indeed. But we are not Jedi, or at least not all of us, and the history of rhetoric is, as a result, both long and complex. Unlike Jedi, we cannot persuade simply by accompanying our words with a wave of the hand. Other methods have been found to accomplish the same goal, which involve the rhetorical use of language. With the successful orator, as with the Jedi, we *want* to conform; we want to go home and rethink our lives. Rhetorical use of language entails the manipulation of words on many levels to make the message convincing and appealing. The levels of persuasion range from the deepest organizational form the argument takes to the particular words chosen to express it. The role of this last, and the place granted colourful, or figurative, language, in making speech persuasive are the aspects I want to look at here.

This book offers a polemical look at rhetoric and the centrality of figurative language in western culture. It is not intended as a survey, like Brian Vickers' *In Defence of Rhetoric*,[1] although its aim is similar in its efforts to present rhetoric as constructive and long lasting. But its purpose differs, as the focus will rest on one aspect of rhetoric, figurative speech, and the way in which the presentation and treatment of this kind of language provide a common denominator among western cultures from the time of Quintilian to the present. The premise of the book is that, in the western tradition, figurative speech – using language to do more than name – provides the main way that language articulates possibility. It argues for a reassertion of the fundamental importance of rhetoric and the acknowledgement that there are embedded 'tropes of possibility' for each culture that offer means of enabling – as well as, admittedly, destroying – the potential of that culture.

Speaking well

Rhetoric is best understood as the way we use words to create community. Cicero, the Roman author, philosopher, and statesman who lived in the first century BCE, claims that rhetoric is the art of *bene dicendi* ('speaking well'); that 'well' should be taken in a variety of senses: speaking correctly, speaking eloquently, but also speaking the good – generating community through language. Speaking well, then, can be extended further to include articulating what that good is, expressing the promise a society offers, from the basic building blocks of the words used in expressing an argument to the structure of the argument itself. Quintilian, the Spanish theoretician of rhetoric writing in the late first century CE, shows how only the good man can speak well, and that those who speak well are essentially good: these include the orators and teachers of rhetoric, as well as those versed in the liberal arts; this is why rhetoric stood at the centre of Roman society from the republic into the empire.

Yet the very prospect of speaking well contains within it a notion that changes with time. If we accept that rhetoric is connected with articulating the good, we must also grant that the representation of that good varies as a culture changes. What is good for Cicero, in republican Rome, is not necessarily so for Quintilian in the imperial world; what these two may share may have nothing to do with how we look at the good now. Since rhetoric, however, posits an equation between speaking and the good, it offers a key to what that good is through the use made of language; as important as *what* people talk about is *how* they talk about it, in terms of both the kinds of arguments they make and the words and phrases they use in making them.

Moreover, the structure of the argument is often condensed into a colourful idiom or habit of speaking, such as, as we shall see, the prevalence of repetition in today's American society, that can point to a culture's concerns. Since the system of figures, or figurative speech, uncovers a culture's habits of seeing, how we view the world and our place in it is revealed through our use of figurative speech, which offers a thumbnail version of the essential angle of the culture and a complex reduction of the limitations and possibilities, a ray of hope – and fear – for that culture.

While it is true that rhetoric has come to be understood as 'slick persuasion', the prevailing Roman definition of the word, 'the art of speaking well', places rhetoric at the heart of any culture where language and ethical action are joined. Yet the pervasiveness of rhetoric is more ingrained than that, for the juncture of language and ethics brings with it a further cluster of burdens and possibilities. Rhetoric, even in its sparest form, that of the treatise, offers a window onto its culture. In their effort to lay down the law most simply, rhetorical treatises tell us about the priorities of a culture that are embedded in their language and linguistic interactions, revealing choices and priorities both in what is said and in what is omitted. Because rhetorical treatises chart the intersection of language and ethics, they reveal more about the culture they spring from than do most didactic works.

A look at rhetorical treatises and their attempts to define figurative speech – especially the places where the types of figures are distinguished – will lead us into a discussion of how the seamless façade of a treatise is often cracked and revealing, enabling the treatise both to codify use and to adumbrate change. Like a trail guide, rhetorical treatises spell out the lay of the land: what each term means, how metaphor differs from simile, and so forth. Yet as with the trail guide, attempts at clarification often lead to a place where description doesn't hold, where the narrative mapping does not match the terrain. Trail guides tend to indicate these points by odd irruptions of unfamiliar terms, sometimes from foreign languages, sometimes through strange comparisons. An infamous section of a trail in the Adirondack mountains of New York, for instance, is described in the standard guidebook in the following words:

> Leaving Bear Den, the trail descends to a col, ascends slightly, and then drops to the main col between Bear Den and Dial mts. at 3.0 mi., having lost 220 ft (67 m.) in altitude. The trail now climbs over one more small bump before beginning the final long climb to the summit of Dial Mt. at 3.8 mi.[2]

Hikers all learn that a 'col' is a valley, but they often learn the hard way; the guide suggests that the valley is something to beware of by the switch from English to French, from straightforward descriptive language to a word that is at once more obscure and more technically precise. Compared to the folksy language that follows, which describes the hill after the valley ('one more small bump'), 'col' jumps out as a trouble spot, both in the text and in the trail. The fact that the guide cannot adequately describe the trail is indicated by these metaphoric means. The same is true of the rhetorical treatise, where the effort to distinguish clearly between terms always at some point fails and descriptive language proves inadequate to the task.

I intend, in short, to look at rhetorical treatises not as how-to manuals but, rather, as indices of cultural values: their didactic nature enables them to illuminate more clearly than other genres the choices and interests of the culture that produced them. But I will also look at literary works as demonstrations of these values, as examples of how they played out in the creative minds of the time.

Why the treatise?

As an attempt at classification, treatises are clearly intended to organize knowledge, for both descriptive and prescriptive purposes: that is, the treatise serves as both a repository of accepted distinctions and a blueprint for future decisions. Because rhetoric is so strongly grounded in ancient thought, it is a particularly conservative example of classification. Nonetheless, it functions as any other how-to manual: each author who writes a rhetorical treatise manipulates the 'inherited classifications, weighting, reordering, and amending them'.[3] Even though the purpose of a treatise is to separate domains – decide what should go where and what is irrelevant – it is never the case that ambiguity is excluded. Thus every rhetorical treatise sets out with the goal of classifying language and ends up, somewhere, failing to do so.

Why this is so strikes me as a fascinating question, for it would seem to dismantle the purpose of the treatise as a whole. Treatises serve to clarify and discern; terms that do not fit clearly in a given category would seem anathema to the notion of a treatise. And yet, as we shall see, every treatise includes these moments of confusion. These two aspects of the treatise function together – the adaptation of inherited classifications and the failure to fully classify – and it is in this space that one is offered a glimpse of the world as it is, or was. The fact that such texts are 'projections, not copies, of reality'[4] requires that the match not be perfect. Rhetorical treatises are charts of cultural assumptions only if they are read with an eye for what is confused; descriptive works, likewise, offer insight if attention is paid to the parts that do not fit the picture or its frame.

If, in sum, rhetorical treatises set out to define the topic clearly, they always fail in the process. But where they fail is where we find what truly matters: what is possible and what is at risk in that culture. In its failure the anomaly will frame a central ambiguity of the culture; that ambiguity points at once toward the culture's highest aspirations and toward its greatest source of weakness. Having set out to guide and clarify, treatises often show how topics resist organization and in the process point toward what a culture deems important if conflicted.

An example of this phenomenon comes from the 2004 movie *Hitch*. Will Smith as Alex Hitchins, or 'Hitch', plays the 'date doctor' who knows all the rules for getting a date but seems to have no luck in finding the perfect love himself. What becomes apparent through the course of the film, however, is that his principles in general don't work, for others as well as for himself. The funniest scene in the movie shows Kevin James assuring the date doctor that dancing is the one area where he needs no coaching. He demonstrates his prowess – 'making the pizza', 'putting it in the oven' – to Hitch's horror; at the end of the dance Hitch states unequivocally that he must *never* 'do that again'. But Hitch turns out to be wrong: it is James' dancing that wins the heart of the heiress he is in love with; as audience we are keyed into this revelation by the disjunction between the rules and the reality, the fact that what is reputedly so wrong is in fact so funny and so appealing. At the end of the film, Hitch – which, as he says, is both a verb and a noun, hovering between the date and its failure – stops himself short and says, 'Basic principles: … There are none.' It is not where the rules fit but where they fail that we glimpse the workings of the culture that lurks behind them.

Figurative language

While Aristotle expends relatively little energy on defining style, focussing more on argument, he does still argue that style can be used for emphasis: he calls this *enargeia*, or bringing before the eyes (*Rhetoric* 10.4; 11.1), suggesting that a figure was granted a power that transcended the one normally associated with speech. His examples from Homer include 'the arrow flew' or 'was eager to fly'; and from more common speech he uses as examples 'you would have thought him a basket of mulberries' to describe someone with a black eye; or 'he has legs like stringy parsley' to describe someone scrawny; in this, he suggests that there is a world beyond that of direct description. While Aristotle did not subdivide this use of language into types of figurative speech, he clearly believed in the power of careful and colourful word choice.

Later, however, style becomes subdivided into different types of figurative language. Much has been written on how the types of figurative language are uncategorizable. Yet similar terms exist in all subsequent rhetorical treatises and are presented in comparable ways. Figures of speech are forms of figurative language that affect the shape of the words; figures of thought are those that do the same with the ideas. Literary examples are often easy to spot: 'Full fathom five my father lies' uses the figure of speech known as alliteration, or using the same sound at the beginning of successive words; while 'I burned my candle at both ends' is an example of metaphor as figure of thought, where the comparison between life and candle is implied rather than spelled out. But figures are prevalent in other media as well: advertising depends on association and so employs figures: the cockney gecko that advertises Geico insurance derives from a pun; its power resides in the play on words even as the lizard plays with the accents of its speech. And idiomatic speech turns on the use of figures: things that are popular are 'sweet', 'wicked', or 'cool' though in reality they have nothing to do with taste, vice, or temperature; country music, like rap music, is rooted in the rhymes and repetitions of speech drawn from spoken idiom: 'all my exes live in Texas'. In every case colourful language causes the argument – the song, the ad, the conversation – to sparkle and be seductive. Throughout the history of rhetoric, for this reason, figurative use of language is referred to as 'colours' or 'bringing speech to life' or 'making language visible'. Figurative speech is lively and playful: it enhances persuasion by making an argument appealing.

The chapters in this book are illustrative rather than comprehensive: I will start with a chapter on contemporary tropes, then move back to Quintilian and his failures of categorization. From there we move to the twelfth century, where two examples in particular will speak to a shift in priority. Finally, there is a chapter on Montaigne. In each case, error leads the way; the assertion of confusion and mistake, of anomaly, speaks to a deeper structural principle. The rhetorical map is not stable. Like the earth's crust, it shifts and moves and the cracks are discernible, bringing with them a trace of what lies beneath.

Strikingly, the figures this method highlights speak to delay of one form or another, a delay that creates a place for ethical action. From Cicero to now, the figure that causes the most trouble to those categorizing seems to frame for the culture the issues that matter most. While the examples may change, the truths they reveal are consistently telling. Rhetoric, as we shall see, is thus remarkable for its consistency and its flexibility, offering a means for comparison as well as an index of differences. Approached both as a prescriptive and as a descriptive system, rhetoric can and does reveal much about a culture as it offers us insight into how a community sees, and so constitutes, itself.

Eric Cheyfitz[5] has argued that figurative language actually serves to create a space between signified and signifier, between what something is and what it is called, and in that space enables the playing out of the dialogue essential to them, as well as to our notion of the power of language to effect change. Cheyfitz's language here is useful, since the spatial effect of figurative language lies at the core of our study. In order for rhetoric to function humanistically it must assume as well as create a space for community. The parameters of that space – and even its location – change over time, as do the forces needed to clear the field, as it were. But in each case, a figure that causes the most trouble in the treatises is one that is linked with the culture's understanding of where the space for discovery lies. In ancient Rome it is the space of the forum; in the medieval texts, it is the space of both performance and text, especially reading; in the early modern texts it is the space of the page; in contemporary parlance it is the space of a sound bite. In each a contradiction arises over the use of this space – be it for dialogue or for control – and this contradiction is apparent in the particular trope that comes to represent the angle of vision. Hesitation and correction mark the space of ancient Rome; dwelling on a point, medieval; chiasm, early modern; repetition, contemporary. In each, expanding beyond denotation marks the angle of vision and the priorities of the culture, which in turn mark the adaptability of rhetoric to its circumstances.

In each instance, then, figurative speech will lead us to a figure that is troubled and that, in turn, maps out the parameters of the goals and pitfalls of its culture. In each case the mapping is literal: a space is opened up that allows for dialogue, whether it is on the macro level of the forum or the micro level of language's refusal to clone. Figurative speech isolates the space the culture envisions for the interchange rhetoric allows; the particular space rhetoric grants for ethical action is indicated by a figure it identifies as its own.

1

Weapons of Mass Creation: Repetition versus Replication

'It's déjà vu all over again'

Our culture copies endlessly: emails, xeroxes, faxes are reproduced at the touch of a button. Cloning, first a fictional conceit, now a reality, places a premium on replication over differentiation. In a recent story, the American fiction writer Ralph Lombreglia alludes to this in a key scene:

> He straightened up and entered the shop. They'd had a productive evening here at Copy Blast. The air was metallic with the ozone-rich exhalations of mechanical reproduction. He felt it in his teeth. Massive acts of duplication had occurred in this place while the rest of the world slept, like a massacre in reverse. They should drive historical markers into the floor, Michael thought, to commemorate what happened here – the nightly mass-murder of all that was unique, singular, one-of-a-kind.[1]

Repetition as anaphora was, in ancient treatises, a form of superficial decoration, a stylistic element added for emphasis. George Kennedy, in his history of western rhetoric, cites repetition as the prime example of figures of speech, or 'changes in the sound or arrangement of a sequence of words, *such as anaphora*'.[2] But in the sign systems of our culture, repetition has migrated from superficial ornamentation to deep structural principle. It has become rooted in the symbols of our society, in our thought patterns. It has progressed from a figure of speech to a figure of thought. It provides a glimpse of what differentiates our era from all others and, as a result, it provides a way in, linguistically: it is a basic building block of our culture.

It is the premise of this book that places where figures shift categories are epistemologically significant. In each instance the key figure is linked to the sign system (or systems) of a culture. While the figure functions on the 'plot' level of a culture's story, it also taps into the deeper symbolic level and reveals how that culture views the relationship between community and language. Moreover, when a trope changes registers, such as from figure of speech to figure of thought, it often seems to indicate a shift in the 'plate tectonics' of the culture.

In *The Vital Illusion* Jean Baudrillard argues that cloning is the 'collective fantasy of a return to a non-individuated existence and a destiny of undifferentiated life'.[3] It is, after all, the goal of cloning to create an exact replica that will therefore undo death. In this, he argues, we are engaged in a 'double and contradictory movement': on the one hand, we want to build a 'deathless alter ego' whose purpose is to perfect natural selection; on the other we want to put an end to natural selection. While our dreams about cloning suggest that we strive toward perfecting existence, the fact of the matter may be otherwise: in cancelling differentiation we also limit possibilities. Our vision becomes blocked by this 'artificial paradise' of technology and virtuality; language as symbolic exchange becomes useless.

And yet language fights back. Baudrillard argues that against the dead end of cloning there remain traces of opacity and mystery apparent in cosmology, best represented in linguistic and poetic terms:

In relations between things there is always a hiatus, a distortion, a rift that precludes any reduction of the same to the same. That is even more true for human beings. We are never exactly present to ourselves, or to others. Thus we are not exactly real for one another, nor are we quite real even to ourselves. And this radical alterity is our best chance – our best chance of attracting and being attracted to others, of seducing and being seduced. Put simply, our chance at life.[4]

20

Science, he argues, and the linearity of science, has it all wrong. 'We are victims of an absence of destiny, of a lack of illusion. ... But it seems that something resists this irresistible trend, something irre-ducible' that lies beyond the completely knowable. 'As a metaphor, I would say that at the core of every human being and every thing there is such a fundamentally inaccessible secret'. [5] This 'vital illu-sion', to borrow Nietzsche's phrase as used by Baudrillard, is best represented by what he calls the 'vernacular' of language: it is this aspect of signing that indicates that reality is always one step removed from itself, that language never signifies what it means. The inaccessible secret is indeed a metaphor, or the concept of metaphor itself. Where science may have had it wrong, language, rhetoric, had it right. Eric Cheyfitz, in the *Poetics of Imperialism*, supports this claim. 'Figurative language ... is the driving force of language itself. For the language within language that is the force of language opens up a space between signified and signifier, a rupture of identity, where the conflictive play of dialogue takes place. ... Eloquence is conceived of both as what makes the polis the free marketplace of ideas ... and, contradictorily enough, as what can mesmerize the other into silent assent'.[6]

It is therefore both surprising and comprehensible that Baudrillard seems to believe that hope lies in the tendency of language to turn to the past, to look back over its shoulder. For Baudrillard this comes from the fact that we no longer possess a forward-looking providential vision. Language – what Baudrillard calls the vernacular, but clearly includes the figurative – offers the truest representation of the secret of our existence. Not only do we sustain illusions through language, we insist on the inability of the subject to identify fully with the object. In humanistic rhetoric the object never can become the subject. On the contrary, the purpose of figures is to insist on a disparity between subject and object. It is, in short, the rhetorical vision that will enable the vital illusion to be sustained.

Baudrillard maintains that the struggle between subject and object forced on us by the technological will to clone is opposed to a classical theory of knowledge. Yet it is not, I would maintain, opposed to a classical theory of rhetoric, which asserts at every turn that the world is knowable only at a remove: that the purpose of the figurative is to capture the illusion at the heart of truth. The prevalence of beginning again and again in the face of society's seeming death-wish to end differentiation suggests that in the arts, at least, an effort at a poetic, or rhetorical, resolution is sustained. The rhetorical turn – the arts of language that persuade in a way that denies the identification of subject and object – insists repeatedly on the necessity of beginning, even as the positivistic sciences push on toward an ending.

Every shift in culture, be it radical or gradual, brings with it a threat that is also a possibility. The possibilities envisioned by modernity, by science, often threaten our sense of humanity. Rhetoric first emerged as the response to one of the earliest versions of this, as the world of fifth-century BCE Greece started to identify itself as Greek, and thus distinguish itself from the *barbaroi*. Yet that distinction – a linguistic distinction at heart – created the possibility for figurative speech and the need for teachers of rhetoric, for those who could use that distinction for social purposes. Writing in the fourth century BCE, Plato is uneasy with the early rhetoricians, which suggests the power they must have had, since, he says, that power lay in their ability to persuade 'without knowledge'. In a famous passage from the *Phaedrus* (266A) he distinguishes two different types of rhetoric:

> As our two discourses just now assumed one common principle, unreason, and then, just as the body, which is one, is naturally divisible into two, right and left, with parts called by the same names, so our two discourses conceived of madness as naturally one principle within us, and one discourse, cutting off the left-hand part, continued to divide this until it found among its parts a sort of left-handed love, which it very justly reviled, but the other discourse, leading us to the right-hand part of madness, found a love having the same name as the first, but divine, which it held up to view and praised as the author of our greatest blessings.[7]

1. Weapons of Mass Creation

While, indeed, rhetoric can be used by people who know what they are talking about, and by those who do not, and while it is indeed true that is possible to persuade an audience either way, it is also true that what matters, finally, is the end result: what is created by the orator's delivery, be it spoken or written. How this end is achieved is perhaps less important than that it is reached at all. On the one hand, rhetoric can create a sense of community and hope; on the other, a climate of fear and hatred. Either rhetoric – Plato's right or left hand – can result in either of these ends, and it is the end result that determines the role of rhetoric in society. Humanistic rhetoric, unlike philosophy, does not deal in the language of truth. Its currency is illusion, yet that illusion is one that, potentially, enables hope, love, seduction, and life.

Tropes of possibility

Rhetoric can and has been approached as a school subject, a topic we learn either for its own sake or as an aid to composition. Yet the fact that the rhetorical treatise, in varied form, has remained vital in every era since Cicero's, and that the use of figurative speech has become an increasingly large part of the discipline of rhetoric, suggests that there is more at work than an academic subject. On the contrary, the analysis of figurative speech – and its centrality – gets at something crucial to our understanding of who we are.

Contemporary work on the theory of figures tends to focus on their place in constructing nationalistic and imperial systems, with particular emphasis placed on the importance of the figurative level as the first marker of deviation from the native norm. By our time, in the world of the global village, differences of this kind are increasingly critical. The smaller the world becomes, the greater importance is placed on difference and individuality; and if the nations are incapable of providing a sense of identity, other subgroups will fill the void. Figures will remain, however, since differentiation, alienation, self-definition by whatever means will persist. As Baudrillard suggests, figures derive from the need to euphemize and create illusion.

23

My argument is both synchronic and diachronic. On the one hand I argue that figures are a fact of our humanity, at least our western mentality, and a good one at that – through a true use and understanding of figurative work we can resist efforts to erode our best and most humane instincts. On the other I suggest that figures shift, constantly, as our attempts to explore our position in the world and through language shift as well. Other efforts to make diachronic arguments of this type seem limited by a sense of how innate figuration is. In her important work on the history of rhetoric, Shirley Sharon-Zisser argues at length about the evolutionist language that is prevalent in nineteenth-century tracts about rhetoric.[8] From this she asserts that rhetoric served to turn its back on the past, to reject the earlier, pre-evolved past of ancient rhetoric. And yet it is also a fact that the very era that produced Darwinian discussion of evolution and the relative lack of importance of the past also produced the archaeological fetishization of the past in many fields, most notably Freud's work on psychoanalysis. It is his metaphor of the mind as an archaeological *Tell* that sets the tone and language for the next decades of psychoanalytical thought and writing. Moreover, Sharon-Zisser's assertion that the nineteenth century, in turning its back on the past, likewise turned its back on the 'binarism' of figures and tropes that so characterized ancient rhetoric is suspect. The split between the two is never as clear-cut as Sharon-Zisser would maintain.

It seems possible to suggest, rather, that the evolutionary language of the nineteenth-century rhetorical treatises spoke to the kind of fear we have seen here: a fear that modernity would erase that which is held most dear, and a certainty that the very expression of that fear as figure will ensure its failure. In articulating the idea that rhetoric is evolutionary, a contradiction is created that can only be overcome through rhetoric. The use of rhetorical terminology that is conservative by nature ensures that modernity will remain at a remove. And yet, there is something that shifts from era to era, something that enables a figure to be more or less entrenched in a culture. It seems hard to sustain the argument that only the ancients felt a difference between these two fields when we ourselves are experiencing just that.

In the end rhetoric is indeed about illusion. Plato was right to be suspicious of it, since its purpose is to move beyond the arguments of reason toward the smoke and mirrors of poetry. Yet in its ability to combine *taxis* and *lexis* – taxonomy and terminology – rhetoric is uniquely qualified to explore our nature, our identity, our being. And of the categories within rhetoric, it is figures that seem most enduring as they try to explain, without being able to escape their own terms, the nature of the central illusion that defines humanity. What that humanity is – which way it faces, how it defines itself – shifts from era to era. Yet it is the uncanny ability of figures to capture and sustain those things we find most central.

My contention, then, is that humanistic discourse of any era devolves from a rhetorical troping – a spinning toward the light – of the perception of truth. The play of illusion – the shifting of registers, the seeming disregard of what is known, or what can be known, or what can be done with what is known – is essential not only to the history of rhetoric itself but, more important, to the representation of humanity that emerges.

Each of the eras looked at in this work is associated with humanistic endeavours; each is also a time of tremendous social change and threats to the very notion of humanity. The truth that was being imposed from without – in the name of empire, religion, science – brought with it a cluster of key concepts. From those concepts a sense of purpose was derived, as was a need to embroider, to play, to shift around the categories a bit. Where those shifts happened – be it from depth to surface, or otherwise – a rift was created that enabled a new rhetorical vision to emerge. This is what I aim to illuminate in this and the following three chapters.

Beginning again

At the beginning of Woody Allen's masterpiece, *Manhattan*, the movie stutters and stumbles, trying to get started:

Chapter One. He adored New York City. He idolized it all out of proportion. No, make that, he *romanticized* it all out of proportion. There. To him, no matter what the season was, this was still a town that existed in black and white and pulsated to the great tunes of George Gershwin. (Uh, no, let me start this over.)

Chapter One. He was too romantic about Manhattan, as he was about everything else. He thrived on the hustle-bustle of the crowds and the traffic. To him, New York meant beautiful women and street-smart guys who seemed to know all the angles. (Nah, corny, too corny for a man of my taste. Let me try to make it more profound.)

Chapter One. He adored New York City. To him, it was a metaphor for the decay of contemporary culture. The same lack of individual integrity that caused so many people to take the easy way out was rapidly turning the town of his dreams into … (it's going to be too preachy … I mean, you know, let's face it, I want to sell some books here).

Chapter One. He adored New York City. Although to him it was a metaphor for the decay of contemporary culture. How hard it was to exist in a society desensitized by drugs, loud music, television, crime, garbage… (too angry … I don't want to be angry).

Chapter One. He was as tough and romantic as the city he loved. Behind his black-rimmed glasses was the coiled sexual power of a jungle cat. (I love this.) New York was his town, and it always would be.

In this opening monologue, as the Gershwin score plays loudly in the background and the camera offers glorious black-and-white shots of Manhattan – particularly of Central Park – the narrator finally reaches the central metaphor of his movie: Manhattan is like a woman, marked by youth or decay, a conceit the movie plays out through Alvie Singer's attraction to the pubescent Mariel Hemingway and the older Diane Keaton. Unclear to the finish which of the two the island really is, the narrator vacillates – sending one off, then the other, returning to first one, then the other – all in a New York minute, or two. Starting over and over, the movie, like its protagonist, seems to insist that it is all about beginning again, replaying with a difference. We have come, in fact, to depend upon beginning again by replaying the central moments of our lives, whether it be through watching videos of our weddings and bar mitzvahs or literally, as in *Manhattan*, starting from scratch with someone different as a way of understanding ourselves. It has become difficult to watch a live sports game precisely because there is no instant replay, no way to go back and, if not fix it, then fix our expectation and understanding of the event by watching the now increasingly present large-screen TV in the corner of the bar. Repetition is by now so ingrained in us that experiences in which it is not an option are disconcerting.

Recently this interest in repetition has taken a particular turn in the media, in the form of the theme of short-term memory loss. Whether it is the beguiling figure of Dory in *Finding Nemo*, Bill Murray in *Groundhog Day*, or Drew Barrymore in *Fifty First Dates*, the theme and message of short-term memory loss are played and replayed in the current cinema. Bill Murray's character in *Groundhog Day* may relive the same day over and over, yet it is always different. Through repetition he finds, finally, the way to Andie MacDowell's heart, and he becomes less of a cad. So, too, in *Fifty First Dates* Drew Barrymore's character moves beyond the prison of her short-term memory as Adam Sandler expands the perimeter of her world. Drew Barrymore is first treated as an invalid by those around her, since she replays the same day over and over; by the end she seems to remember what is important – to turn on the video that will bring her up to speed; to recognize the fact that she is married; etc. – without being weighed down by anxiety and fear. For Dory in *Finding Nemo* the fact that she cannot remember past a few sentences – at least at the start – seems to be a release: unlike the clownfish Marlin, she does not become overwhelmed by memory and so anxiety; she is the risk-taker of the two. Even when she starts to remember things as she seems to become attached to Marlin, her lack of a past is freeing, both for her and for those she is with. That the past is a dead weight on our shoulders is of course a myth; that the inability to remember it is somehow possible and liberating is also a myth, yet it seems to be one with which we are increasingly fascinated.

Significantly, these are repetitions that defy cloning – repetitions with a difference – and, as such, they speak to the ingrained nature of repetition in our industrial society even as they indicate how the trope of repetition with a difference has become essential to our creative landscape. Because we can repeat ourselves precisely, we must repeat ourselves; yet that repetition need not end difference. Perhaps the most compelling example of precisely this phenomenon is the 2004 movie *The Eternal Sunshine of the Spotless Mind*. Named after a line in a poem about Abelard and Heloise by Alexander Pope – the line speaks of the purity of the vestal virgins – the movie creates a world without rhetoric: a world in which language casts no shadows at all. Here technology, at the firm called 'Lacuna', is employed to erase not just memories but also one's emotional core. A map is made of the brain, and from that map areas of emotional disturbance are eradicated, presumably leaving one happier. The characters then relive their lives, devoid of remembered painful conflict. Life becomes a constant tape of itself, and we are shown what would happen if all difference – and all conflict – were erased. Yet the movie ends with the protagonists escaping the Möbius strip of their lives as they figure out a way not to escape – 'What if you stay this time?' – not to rewind the tape and live without conflict. The edifice of their repetitive life avoiding conflict crumbles as they seek to escape from repetition and mind-numbing boredom and strike out on their own. It is, in the end, their refusal to relive banality that saves them. Repetition that is only cloning, only replication, is shown to be deadening, while repeating lives with difference embedded becomes worthwhile.

1. Weapons of Mass Creation

It is this power of repetition with a difference that lies at the heart of another movie, *Memento* (directed by Christopher Nolan and based on a short story by his brother, Jonathan, called *Memento Mori*). The movie is told in reverse: the protagonist, Leonard Shelby, who has short-term memory loss brought on by the traumatic death of his wife, gradually reveals to us and to himself how we know what we know. Strikingly, knowledge for him is rooted in repetition in two distinct forms: everyone, he asserts, should be able to learn things through conditioning and repetition; it is habit and routine that make life possible. The movie draws on the urban myth of a man who remembered things by keeping notes to himself in the pockets of his suit, only to become hopelessly confused by their lack of order. Here the protagonist has a system: to transfer the crucial notes to tattoos on his body. Memory thus becomes reified as corporeal text and meaning is created through rereading and interpretation. He trusts his handwriting, he says, and he trusts the writing on his hand. Memory is ordered, a system is created through linking language and the body that explains not who we are but how we understand the world, our habit of looking.

In a key flashback between the protagonist and his wife, she is shown reading a thick book. The book is never named: what matters rather is the discussion the two have about the fact that she has read and reread the book, which makes no sense to the protagonist:

> Leonard: How can you read that again?
> Leonard's wife, without looking up: It's good.
> Leonard: You've read it a hundred times.
> Leonard's wife: I enjoy it.
> Leonard: Yeah, but the pleasure of a book is in wanting to know what happens next.

And yet it is precisely through rereading – his notes, his tattoos – that the protagonist is able to sort out what has happened, to remember. Memory, he says, is not facts: you cannot be bullied into remembering. Memory, instead, is interpretation: 'Memory can change the shape of a room or the color of a car. It's an interpretation, not a record.' The process of rereading is a process of repetition, then, with a difference: interpretation creates memory.

Throughout, images are set against text: the protagonist carries Polaroids – photographs without negatives – with him. The difference between original and copy was initially signalled by the language of opposition: the negative was the original, the print, or positive, was the copy. Yet even here language makes clear our valuation of the two stages: the original was less useful to us – hence negative – than the copy, the print, the positive, the one we kept in our albums. Now, of course, the system is in the process of changing: digital cameras, like Polaroids, only have copies; there is no negative to start from. Yet what we find is that the endless stream of digital prints is manipulated to produce collages or virtual movies: it is the way we can play with and change the sameness that becomes important. Again, because we can make exact copies our instinct is to play off the precision and focus on alteration. Repetition is still key to our lexicon and understanding; yet, as Lombreglia and Baudrillard make clear, exact repetition replicates little that is living. Because language derives from difference, and rhetorical language depends on a subtle play of identity and alteration, it is rhetoric that captures for our culture, as for all the others looked at here, the essence of that culture. Precisely because rhetoric is the mapping of the virtual illusion, the fact that the subject is not the object and never will be, rhetoric has become increasingly important and prominent in our culture. Not only has repetition migrated from a stylistic flourish to a deep cultural trope, but rhetoric itself has surfaced as the means to retain our sense of vitality.

For what matters to Leonard Shelby is the fact that the annotations on each Polaroid tell him how to treat this person pictured there. Rereading enables meaning, and word and action coincide in the tattooed body of the protagonist and the annotated images he carries. As Allegra Goodman writes in her essay on reading *Pride and Prejudice,*

I think unfolding is what rereading is about. Like pleated fabric, the text reveals different parts of its pattern at different times. And yet every time the text unfolds, in the library, or in bed, or upon the grass, the reader adds new wrinkles. Memory and experience press themselves into each reading so that each encounter informs the next.[9]

Umberto Eco's novel, *The Mysterious Flame of Queen Loana (La Misteriosa Fiamma della Regina Loana)*, makes this point exactly:

You can't think of memory as a warehouse where you deposit past events and retrieve them later just as they were when you put the there. ... I don't want to get too technical, but when you remember something, you're constructing a new profile of neuronal excitation ... you reactivate that initial pattern of neuronal excitation with a profile of excitation that's similar to but not the same as that which was originally stimulated. Remembering will therefore produce a feeling of unease. In short, to remember is to reconstruct, in part on the basis of what we have learned or said since.[10]

In this novel the protagonist, again, loses his short-term memory; yet, unlike the protagonist in *Memento*, he cannot remember who he is, even though he can remember everything he has ever read. That, however, does not help him regain his sense of self: what works is a visit to his family home, in whose attic he uncovers texts that help him reconstruct his life: in rereading he 'remembers' who he is. But the core of his self-discovery remains the recovery of his first love: with that, he will be able to reconstruct his life. Again love surfaces, as in *Memento*, as central to self, but here love is the basis for language: it is the subject rather than the object of being. The protagonist's first love, whose face he strives to recall, is melded with the heroine whose name provides the title of the book, and who was, herself, the heroine of a comic book from his past:

31

You read any old story as a child, and you cultivate it in your memory, transform it, exalt it, sometimes elevating the blandest thing to the status of myth. In effect, what seemed to have fertilized my slumbering memory was not the story itself, but the title. The expression *the mysterious flame* had bewitched me, to say nothing of Loana's mellifluous name, even though she herself was a capricious little fashion plate dressed up as a *bayadère*. I had spent all the years of my childhood – perhaps even more – cultivating not an image but a sound. Having forgotten the 'historical' Loana, I had continued to pursue the oral aura of other mysterious flames. And years later, my memory in shambles, I had reactivated the flame's name to signal the reverberation of forgotten delight.[11]

The Mysterious Flame, in which the loss of memory is gradually replaced by a flood of memories, centres on the ascent of a Gorge through a needle-like slit in the fog that becomes the pivotal scene in the novel, as the protagonist gradually reconstructs his encounter with death there in the reconstitution of his memory. Yet his true drive – to see again the face of his first love, his Beatrice (the book is, in many ways, a reading of Dante's *Divine Comedy*) – provides the concluding climax ('I...feel on the verge of orgasm, as my brain's corpora cavernosa swell with blood, as something gets ready to explode – or blossom'[12]) of the novel as the apocryphal flood of unorganized memory culminates in the apocalyptic final lines: 'I feel a cold gust, I look up. Why is the sun turning black?'.[13] Memory is provoked through rereading, and through this the protagonist is granted a second chance:

Now, as on that day in the foyer, I am finally about to see Lila, who will descend still modest and mischievous in her black smock, lovely as the sun, white as the moon. ... She will descend like the first frost, and will see me, and will gently extend her hand, not in invitation but simply to keep me from fleeing once again.

32

I will finally learn how to perform forevermore the final scene of my *Cyrano*, I will see what I have looked for all my life … and I will be reunited. I will be at peace.[14]

'The final scene of his *Cyrano*' is the moment when language and desire are united, when rejection is overcome by rhetoric. It is the culmination of a rereading that enables a new performance, one in which the verbally clever is identified with the good through love.

'Don't look back!'

The flipside of this expectation can be demonstrated by reports from 9/11. When the North Tower was hit, according to reports at the time, the impact was processed as a bomb, a replay of the 1993 bombing of the Twin Towers. It wasn't until the South Tower was hit seventeen minutes after the North that the attack was understood on its own terms. As reported in the *9/11 Commission Report*, 'the prospect of another plane hitting the second building was beyond the contemplation of anyone giving advice. According to one of the first fire chiefs to arrive, such a scenario was unimaginable, 'beyond our consciousness'.[15] The South Tower was not evacuated after the North Tower was hit, since 'no one appears to have thought a second plane could hit the South Tower' (p. 317). The second event has come to validate and identify the first, not the other way around; without the second the first is often misconstrued.

When the towers fell the phrase repeated was 'Don't look back!' In the flurry of media attempts to make sense of what had happened, of how the attack would affect our perspective and our lives, it was posited, by Roger Rosenblatt and others, that the age of irony had ended. Given that irony in its most basic form means to say one thing and mean another – in other words, that irony is the quintessential rhetorical figure – it seems fitting that the feared end of irony would be signalled by the repeated phrase, 'Don't look back'. As we shall see, for Quintilian figurative speech is characterized by the action of looking back: the fact is we did look back – over and over, to other terrorist attacks, to the falling – and fallen – buildings themselves, even as the buildings themselves looked to each other for meaning. Irony did not end there; understanding of our culture continues to place figurative language at its centre.

The conviction that surfaced on 9/11 – that irony was dead – was undone by the very repetition of the act itself. We fear, always, that irony will die; we fear that the machines, or the terrorists, will keep us from encountering the world on terms that render it meaningful, and yet we keep making sense of ourselves and others. It is the deep and abiding power of figurative speech that it captures the ineffable at our core. As a result rhetoric is the system most able to express our fears and desires, to present us as we see ourselves, and figurative speech grants the parameters of the era to that image. The central image points at the central fear of a culture even as it demonstrates how that fear is incapable of destroying us.

Stanley Fish's lucid account of the importance of irony to post-modern culture makes this point succinctly:

> If you mean [by objective] a standard of validity and value that is independent of any historically emergent and therefore revis-able system of thought and practice, then it is true that many postmodernists would deny that any such standard is or could ever be available. But if by 'objective' one means a standard of validity and value that is backed up by the tried-and-true proce-dures and protocols of a well-developed practice or discipline … then such standards are all around us. … What this means…is that…there is no *public space*, complete with definitions, stan-dards, norms, criteria, etc., to which one can have recourse in order to separate out the true from the false, the revolutionary from the criminal. And what *that* means is that there is no common ground … that would allow someone or some body to render an independent judgment.[16]

There is no single truth. Instead, there are standards, protocols that derive from a consensus of those who are informed. These standards take the form of expectations, and are expressed in both vernacular and figurative terms. The very nature of postmodernism is predicated on the centrality not only of irony, but of rhetorical truth: given this setting and this understanding of who and what we are, these are the possibilities offered by rhetorical language.

Weapons of mass creation

The best negative example of the figure of repetition is provided by the Fox network as it is portrayed in the documentary *Outfoxed*. This film argues that Fox uses the trappings of other news networks to promulgate propaganda. Again and again the documentary argues that the Fox sets are modelled after those of other networks, yet the language and arguments are used to promote fear and bias. Through its slogans, its graphics, and its staging, Fox establishes the expectation of objective news reporting only to deliver something quite different. Examples abound: the ticker along the bottom, which we as viewers are trained to see as containing news headlines, includes instead sensationalist tidbits and an ongoing counter of the days left until 2 November 2004 – not election day, but the day 'George W. Bush will be reelected', a sentiment repeated by the newscasters at various intervals. *Outfoxed* interviews former employees, who reveal a variety of similar strategies: one spoke of the use of a segment he designed, 'News Alert' (which was intended to present breaking news, such as Columbine), to speak instead of Martha Stewart's arrest, or J.Lo's marriage. The juxtaposition of items intended to encourage trust and present objectivity with messages that are rooted in opinion serves two purposes: on the one hand, it elevates the level of the mundane; on the other, it erodes our faith in the news process. Where persuasion has been and continues to exist in other venues for humanistic ends, the co-option of the rhetorical form for anti-rhetorical ends obliterates our trust in the media. The shouting of Bill O'Reilly and the ongoing assault from the other shows on the Fox network speak to such erosion. Those who have used the form to anti-humanistic ends have undone what could be the most effective means for promoting rhetoric. 'What amazes me', one editor says, 'is the repetition.' The replay Fox relies on – the use of repetition referred to throughout the film as the 'echo effect' – bludgeons the audience into passivity rather than opening them out to possibility and action. Rather than being 'fair and balanced', as their motto has it, *Outfoxed* argues that Fox reports opinion rather than fact, relying often on the phrase 'some people say' to suggest a source where none exists.

This needs to be stated more boldly still. The attempt to define an era brings with it the ability to destroy it. Baudrillard's discussion of cloning makes this point succinctly. Michael Moore's *Fahrenheit 9/11* supports this reading. Offering countless examples from the 'war on terror', which Moore interprets as a war against the American people fought through the language of hatred and fear, Moore argues that 9/11 was used as a catalyst to sustain the status quo. The war in Iraq, tenuously connected to the attacks of September 11, Moore argues, used – and continues to use – the oppressed of the US to conquer the people of Iraq in an effort to control their oilfields, which in turn will support not the American economy so much as the lifestyles of the rich and famous. *Fahrenheit 9/11*, composed almost entirely of clips from the media, pits the anti-rhetoric of fear against the rhetoric of hope. Moore frames these clips in a collage of hope, or hope gone awry. He points to what he believes rhetoric could do, even as he argues again and again that the same tools have been used to opposite ends. The weapons of mass destruction are presented as, in essence, the anti-rhetoric, the abuse of language and truth, the language of fear and hatred that Bush and vice president Cheney's speeches delivered to the American people. Where rhetoric can provide weapons of mass inspiration or creation, Moore suggests, propaganda can only destroy.

The sound bites that Moore weaves together to create his documentary are fuelled, of course, by our culture's trope of repetition. Yet repetition, he argues again and again, can be deadening if unchanged: the repetition of Bush saying 'We're going to smoke them out', 'smoke them out', 'smoke them out', a phrase shown itself to be a quotation from a Western, has the effect of gunfire, not fireworks.

1. Weapons of Mass Creation

The difference between propaganda and rhetoric is that rhetoric, humanistic rhetoric, insists on the prevailing human spirit. It is a discourse rooted in community, and it is at work turning the new defining trope into a fertile source of further discourse and action. Repetition, though made central by technology and key itself to the development of cloning, is, in the hands of those who approach it rhetorically, a fertile seedbed of possibility. Repetition when used rhetorically today becomes a powerful tool of future-oriented possibility. The 2003 movie *Love Actually* makes this point exactly: the opening premise of the movie is that the newspapers all speak of terrorism and hatred while all around we see love prevailing. The end of the movie, shot at an airport, shows encounter after encounter, not of terrorist cells, or hostage situations, but of reunions. The final frame of the movie multiplies into an infinity of smaller frames picturing people reuniting at airports. The image is not replicated but duplicated; repetition is here a source of burgeoning of life and love, and of difference. The actual is distinguished from the virtual, and love prevails.

The rhetorical figures that surface in each era, the figures that give us a glimpse of the culture and allow us a way in to its centre, as different as they may be, share this quality of hope; the figures that escape definition and lead us toward the heart of a culture are figures that invite us to pause, to step back from the action, to take a look. If figures bring things to life, it is in their ability to create a vantage point from which we can look on. This habit of looking may change in detail with each era; it nonetheless always offers a space, a pause, a place for possibility to emerge. Rhetoric, and figures, capture that space and preserve it, offering a way to escape and start over. Figurative language not so much provokes action as delays it as it speaks to the central concerns of a culture. Rhetoric is the art of speaking well; it offers up a model of possibility that captures the best of a culture and the people within it. It also reveals that culture's greatest weakness. Figures of speech that themselves function figuratively offer a glimpse of that community and what makes it unique.

2

Looking Back: Figures of Speech and Thought in the Roman World

Today, the term 'rhetoric' conjures up images of used-car salesmen and presidential candidates. In ancient Rome, rhetoric was a technical term of particular, if changing, definition, serving, at least from the republic through the empire, as the primary defining social institution. The first simile in Vergil's epic of the Roman empire (first century BCE), the *Aeneid* 1.148-53, suggests as much:

> Just as when, in a large crowd, riots often break out, and the common crowd rages in its mind, and even now torches and rocks fly: rage proffers arms; then if, by chance, they spot a man, well liked and responsible, they fall silent and prick up their attention; he calms their minds with words and softens their hearts.

Here, likening the god of the sea, Neptune, to a Roman orator, Vergil asserts the centrality of the power of speech and oration – where one person can calm and control a raging mob by means of his oratorical skill.

It is difficult for us to imagine an equivalent to this in our society, although the media – especially movies and TV – seem to perform a comparable function for us, given that much of our sense of ourselves derives from these sources. And to the extent that we define ourselves – the way we see ourselves – in terms of relationships played out in the media, this too finds a parallel in ancient rhetoric. Founded in Sicily, or so Plato tells us, by Corax and Tisias, rhetoric was first codified most extensively by Aristotle in his *Rhetoric*.

39

Clearly a treatise of civic interaction as much as a definition of the
means by which a democratic *polis* might best function, Aristotle's
Rhetoric bequeathed to the western tradition a sense that rhetoric
was associated with order and the rational functioning of society.

It is in republican Rome, and really in the hands of Cicero, that the
discipline of humanistic rhetoric comes into its own. In part this is
because Cicero was one of the first to blend the teachings of Aristotle
and Plato; in part it is because Cicero was able to cast rhetoric as the
defining art of the culture: where literature – epic and elegy, in
particular – will define the conflicts of Augustan Rome, Ciceronian
rhetoric, with its articulation of protohumanistic values, encapsu-
lates the priorities of the republican era; the values of republican
Rome find their expression in the treatises and speeches of Cicero. In
the hands of Cicero that programme was extended to suggest that, at
least in republican Rome, a good orator was a good man. As Ann
Vasaly notes:

Cicero defines the man in terms of his accomplishment as an
orator. He contends that if a man is a skilled orator, he proves
himself to be a *vir bonus* [good man] as well, since this skill is,
first of all, motivated by the noble desire to achieve glory and
serve the state, and, second, it is perfected only by study and
training so disciplined and rigorous that it leaves no opportu-
nity for moral corruption.[1]

In turn, the discipline of rhetoric finds its home in the public life
of the pre-imperial world. Laurent Pernot writes that 'the ancient
Roman model is an orator who speaks with careful consideration and
who counts on his status – age, nobility, prestige – to guarantee the
worth of his words. ... he is listened to not so much for his words in
themselves but for his position in the city'.[2] The history of rhetoric
is, to a large extent, the history of the adaptation of these Roman
values. One cannot talk about rhetoric, or use rhetoric, without, on
some level, evoking ancient Rome, and not Rome the great imperial
force but Rome as Cicero defines it, as a unique location in time and

place in which the defining characteristic of Rome is its emphasis on the intersection of language and moral action, best exemplified by the statesman. As Cicero asserts in *De Re Publica*, 'those who rule ... by wise counsel and authority are to be deemed far superior ... to those who take no part at all in the business of government' (1.2.3).[3]

Cicero's understanding of rhetoric as the art of speaking well lies at the heart of both Roman republican *mores* and, somewhat adapted, those of the early empire. The values that Cicero's rhetorical treatises outline – the importance of using Latin correctly; the ability of language to calm and organize a mob; the identification of language with power and authority through its deployment by the statesman – all speak to key values of the Roman republic, which include the ability to use the Latin language in such a way that the values of the Roman life are captured by it: what the orator enacts in his active life he describes in his oratorical representations of that life and, most important, exemplifies in the structure and order of his speech. Speaking of ancient rhetoric in general, Thomas Habinek writes 'mastery of rhetorical speech united communities small and large'.[4]

But Cicero also insists that both the speech itself and the oratorical process follow a particular path. As he says in the *De Oratore*, the orator must 'first hit upon what to say; then manage and marshal his discoveries, not merely in orderly fashion, but with a discriminating eye for the exact weight ... of each argument; next go on to array them in the adornments of style; after that keep them guarded in his memory; and in the end deliver them with effect and charm' (1.31.142-3).[5] Even as developing an argument goes through a set number of stages, from discovery to delivery, so the speech will have a set number of parts, from introduction to conclusion. The fact that these two mirror each other is no coincidence: in each instance the ordering process inherent in rhetorical argument takes over, and much as the final speech is the result of careful planning and execution, so the final persuasion is the result of careful argument through the course of the speech, each of which exemplifies the moral ordering of both speaker and audience.

To study humanistic rhetoric, then, is, at least on some level, to study the adaptation of these Roman republican values by later cultures. While rhetoric had come into being centuries before, it underwent a transformation in the hands of Cicero. For the Greeks before him, rhetoric was a means of persuasion linked, at least in Plato's works, dubiously with the origins of democracy. From Isocrates Cicero borrows the notion that rhetoric is the art of speaking well. For Isocrates, as later for Aristotle, that art was a question of presentation; the 'well' referred to the superficial level of the presentation. Starting with Cicero, *bene* became linked with ethical and moral choices: speaking well means more than speaking correctly. Instead, speaking well means to speak the good and to do so by fashioning your speech in such a way that it reflects the good. Style is linked with content, and both are vehicles for social order and the creation of community.

If rhetoric lay at the heart of the republic, it is easy to see why it continued to be important into the empire. Augustus' Janus-faced move of turning back to the *mos maiorum* (ways of the past) while shifting the groundwork of that system is well documented. Since rhetoric was the keystone of republican society, rhetoric remained central to Augustus' programme even as the role of the orator changed drastically as the need for speeches declined, creating, as Tacitus points out in the *Dialogus*, a loss of real political stakes. In fact, a strange glissage occurred between the ideals of Cicero and Augustus – so at odds during the civil wars – that enabled the Ciceronian understanding of rhetoric as the art of speaking well to endure into the early empire and, to a certain degree, become identified with it. When Vitruvius wrote his architectural treatise under Augustus it not only followed a Ciceronian model, it suggested that the Ciceronian model of order was alive and well under the empire. Cicero describes the origins of rhetoric, and by extension, the *mores* of the republic in the following way:

Moreover, if we wish to consider the origin of this thing we call eloquence – whether it be an art, a study, a skill, or a gift of nature – we shall find that it arose from most honourable

42

causes and continued on its way from the best of reasons. For there was a time when men wandered at large in the fields like animals and lived on wild fare; they did nothing by the guidance of reason, but relied chiefly on physical strength; there was as yet no ordered system of religious worship nor of social duties; no one had seen legitimate marriage nor had anyone looked upon children whom he knew to be his own; nor had they learned the advantages of an equitable code of law. And so through their ignorance and error blind and unreasoning passion satisfied itself by misuse of bodily strength, which is a very dangerous servant.

At this juncture a man – great and wise I am sure – became aware of the power latent in man and the wide field offered by his mind for great achievements if one could develop this power and improve it by instruction. Men were scattered in the fields and hidden in sylvan retreats when he assembled and gathered them in accordance with a plan; he introduced them to every useful and honourable occupation, though they cried out against it at first because of its novelty, and then when through reason and eloquence they had listened with greater attention, he transformed them from wild savages into a kind and gentle folk (*De Inventione* 1.1.2).[6]

Writing years later, Vitruvius describes the origins of architecture, and with it the imperial code, in strikingly similar terms:

Humans, by their most ancient custom, were born like beasts in the woods, and caves, and groves, and eked out their lives by feeding on rough fodder. During that time, in a certain place, dense, close-growing trees stirred by stormy winds and rubbing their branches against one another, took fire. Terrified by the flames, those who were in the vicinity fled. Later, however, approaching more closely, when they discovered that the heat of fire was a great advantage to the body, they threw logs into it and preserving it by this means they summoned others, showing what benefits they had from this thing by means of gestures. In this gathering of people, as they poured forth their breath in varying voices, they established words by happening upon them in their daily routines. Later, by signifying things with more frequent practice, they began by chance occurrence to speak sentences and thus produced conversations among themselves. The beginning of association among human beings, their meeting and living together, thus came into being because of the discovery of fire (*De Architectura*, book 2, chapter 1).[7]

What Augustus took from Cicero – what history grants to Augustus – was an identification between rhetoric and stability and so an affiliation with the ideals of the empire. The orators (and propagandists) who thrived under Augustus, including the emperor himself, were orators who asserted Cicero's plan of identifying goodness with correctness and truth with language. Through a wonderful sleight of hand, Cicero's origin myth became adapted by Augustus through Vitruvius and others, and the notion that speech can generate the good became a cornerstone of the imperial project, even if the actual role of the orator had changed.

Figures of speech and thought

Today, people's lives no longer turn around argument in the same way as they did in ancient Rome. Process toward a desirable goal is seen perhaps in terms of physique or wealth, but not in terms of the power of language to order our thoughts and so our selves and our societies. Closer perhaps to the rhetoric of old is the effect of images, both in advertising and more generally in the media, on our ideals, but this does not involve, nor does it grant the same power to, language in the same way. Yet, as we have seen in the first chapter, notions of the good are certainly not absent from our lives, even as language is not divorced from representing them. Although argument is no longer central to our culture, rhetoric persists through the one element from the ancient system that still pertains: style.

Cicero distinguishes two types of style, one 'simple and concise', the other 'elevated and abundant' (*Brutus*, 201). As Peter Dixon points out, 'underlying this contrast of styles is a contrast between two different uses of language, as a means of communication and as a vehicle of feeling and imagination'.[8] The focus on style came to include a study of how language could do more than name, and the study of style became integrated into the argument. That is, with the realization that word-choice could represent and enhance the nuances of the argument through repeated words and phrases, making comparisons, echoing other speeches, etc., the study of style became seen as an aspect integral to the argument.

These elements of style are known as figures. The 'smallest structural units of rhetorical stylistics'[9] or 'formal phenomena of language beyond the grammatical primary structure',[10] figures have been 'constitutive elements in all kinds of texts from antiquity to the present'. Within the history of rhetorical treatises, figures are notorious for the complex taxonomies they demand; and these taxonomies change shape and definition more often than Proteus. In ancient texts the presence and theory of figures are first presented as a secondary phenomenon: the main structure of the argument needs to be clothed, the lifeless body of the speech needs to be brought to life. This process takes different forms depending on the context, the genre, and, most important, the assumptions of the audience; 'the use and recognition of figures require culturally generated knowledge'.[11] Yet more than any other aspect of rhetoric, the theory of figures continues unabated from the republic to modern times, sometimes in conjunction with other more general rhetorical treatises, sometimes separated out on its own. The theory of figures thus constitutes a system that is as stable as it is flexible; more than any other aspect of rhetoric, including sections of a speech, or training and performance of the orator, the theory of figures bears traces of the heritage of rhetoric while demanding and allowing adaptation to the situation in which it finds itself. It is a system of classification that is 'only moderately stable, but nevertheless tradition-forming'.[12]

The concept of adapting language to say more than it denotes was identified early in the tradition – Gorgias is credited with isolating this – yet the term *figura* does not show up until much later. Used in this sense by Cicero, it is not yet there a technical term; at times he refers to the same phenomena as *lumina orationis, conformatio verborum, conformatio sententiarum* (lights of speech, shape of words, shape of thoughts).[13] Quintilian, however, in a passage we will examine at length, uses the term in this technical sense and solidifies it through quotations drawn from Cicero. Because of this, Cicero is associated throughout the tradition with the theory of figures; any treatise on figures will make reference to the presence of Cicero.

Throughout the tradition figures fall into two categories, figures of speech, which are 'breaks in the normal sentence pattern', and figures of thought, which 'relate to the conduct of thoughts, not words or sentence construction'.[14] In some treatises a third class is introduced, that of tropes, yet 'the constant factor of both models is the subdivision into figures of expression ... and figures of thought'.[15] As such, the theory of figures relies on the assumption that rhetoric is constituted of surface and deep structure. In some theorists' eyes, the surface appeal draws the audience into the content; in the eyes of others it distracts the audience from the seriousness of the matter at hand. For all, however, figures are the aspect of rhetoric that is transferable, from forum to classroom, from state to church, from composition to hermeneutics.

It is, therefore, to the system of figures that we turn, not to provide our own taxonomy, or to debate the difference between figures of thought and tropes, but rather, to approach the system as a cultural grid: to see in the conservative nature of the concept of the taxonomy the places where that effort at categorization falls apart and the anomalies of the culture shine through. For if figures themselves depend upon 'culturally generated knowledge', it would follow that the arrangement of those figures might point toward the values of the culture. What is considered superficial, what deep, will surely change, even as the understanding of *bene* shifts with time. The figures that I have isolated here are all ones that the treatises present as anomalous for one reason or another: they do not fit readily into a distinction between surface and depth. As such, they tell us something about the culture that cannot easily name them.

Quintilian's figures: looking back

Since rhetoric began as a form of public argument, it has always linked language with the body – one need think only of Sam Waterston's career-making performances on *Law and Order* to realize just how dramatic oratorical argument is. Cicero's assertion that language is an ordering force includes within it an unquestioned link between body, language, and power. Whereas Aristotle speaks of figures as bringing a speech before your eyes, Cicero, from his earliest works onwards, casts the speech as a body, and the role of figures as related to the shape and state of that body. There is a significant elision here between the speaker and his speech: for Cicero the two are compared through the body. That is, while the speaker in Cicero's rhetoric is clearly described as present – his gestures, his tone of voice, even his appearance are all part of the art of persuasion – the speech too takes on qualities of the body: it is not only visible, with a beginning, middle, and end, but it has a top and bottom, a head and foot. The correlation between speech and speaker derives from Cicero's firm belief that the speech makes the man, and vice versa: speech and speaker are united in the field of the body, and the better the speech, the better the speaker.

By the first century CE rhetoric was a way to hold onto the past by reading and imitating earlier writers. This fact is perhaps clearest with Quintilian (*c.* 30-95 CE). His *Institutio Oratoria* gives an overview of the education of an orator, from childhood to maturity. Divided into twelve books, it discusses first the training of the orator and the development of a speech. It is, as Pernot points out, 'organized in accordance with the five parts of rhetoric ... even as it regroups these elements into two blocks that basically correspond to content and form respectively'.[16]

Quintilian is particularly interested in the problem of moral value, and his focus, in the final books of the *Institutes*, explores the relationship between morality and style. In this, he turns frequently to Cicero and often seems to be responding directly to him. Where Cicero had worked to create an analogy between the body of the orator and the body of the speech, Quintilian asserts that they are one and the same:

> So the first point to consider is what we should understand by 'Figure'. The word is used in two senses. In one, it means any shape in which a word is expressed – just as our bodies, in whatever pose they are placed, are inevitably in *some* sort of attitude. In the second sense … it means a purposeful deviation in sense or language from the ordinary simple form: the analogy is now with sitting, bending forwards, or looking back (*Institutio Oratoria* 9.1.11).[17]

Drawing on what was for Cicero only a comparison between text and body, Quintilian converts it to an identification: for him the body of the speech is the only body that matters. He goes one step further, though, and insists, in a way that Cicero does not, that the purpose of figurative speech is to bring that body to life: 'This is where the movement and action of oratory are to be found; without these things it is dead, and there is no breath, as it were, to animate the corpse' (9.2.5-6).

In another passage Quintilian points out that

> changes of expression and glances of the eyes are powerful elements in pleading; but if a speaker never stopped pulling extraordinary faces and showing his nervousness by constantly varying his expression and eye movement, he would be a laughing-stock. Oratory too has, as it were, its natural face, which must of course not be fixed in motionless rigidity, but still should normally be kept looking as nature intended it (9.3.101-2);

and again:

It may not seem that the Figure in which something is said is at all relevant to the validity of the Proof, but in fact it lends our words credibility... . If face and eyes and hands can do a lot to move men's minds, how much more can the face of the spoken word, as it were, do for us, when it is set to produce the effect we want! (9.1.21).

In this Quintilian retains Cicero's notion that the speech is like the orator, but he adapts it in a very particular way: the orator is made present in the form of the speech itself through the use of figurative speech. Drawing on Cicero's assertion that figures are essential in establishing the continuity of the good between form and content, and therefore essential to the power of rhetoric, Quintilian likewise grants tremendous importance to figures. For Quintilian, however, figures serve to adapt the earlier model to his new circumstances without losing any of the connection with the Ciceronian ideal. By saying that figures bring a speech to life, Quintilian argues that figures are what makes a speech part of the rhetorical system, are what imbues them with the ordering function Cicero has isolated. Through figures Cicero – and the Ciceronian ideal – is made present.

It is, I would suggest, for this reason that Quintilian quotes Cicero at such length on figures, for figures come for Quintilian to embody the essential Cicero – they contain within them the key to Cicero's view of rhetoric as well as, in Quintilian's characterization of them as life force, adapting them to the disappearance of the orator. It is a striking fact that Quintilian goes only to Cicero for this: Isocrates and, later, Aristotle talked at length about the importance of figurative speech. Yet Quintilian, who does not hesitate to cite the Greeks when he needs or wants to, here turns only to Cicero, suggesting that the story of figurative speech, for the Latin tradition, begins with Cicero. In this Quintilian's moves are strikingly parallel to those of Tiberius' relationship to Augustus. As current research has shown, what has been traditionally perceived as the 'Tiberian trough' of relatively low productivity during the second emperor's reign[18] can in fact be interpreted as a conservative and stabilizing move aimed at ensuring that imperial goals and purposes were entrenched and solidified, as well as a framing move, where the few gestures Tiberius made were aimed at informing the future how to read the monuments and actions of Augustus. In the same way, Quintilian ensures through his significant dependence on Cicero's treatises that the rhetorical programme Cicero laid out remains intact, even as he guides us with his revisionary gaze on how to understand that programme in a more general, less republican context. The identification Cicero made between speaking well and being good becomes an identification between style and morals through Quintilian's treatment of figures.

Figures, then, surface in the Roman rhetorical tradition not as adornments to a speech, an afterthought, but as the very basis of rhetoric itself – its lifeblood. Figures become associated with Cicero, and figures become the part of rhetoric that is most readily transmitted through the ages. Yet Quintilian offers us one further item that deserves analysis. His quotation of Cicero cited above centres on one particular aspect of figures: the inclination of tradition to divide them into figures of speech, figures of thought, and tropes. Like Quintilian, Cicero believes that the only meaningful distinction is the first one, that of figures of speech and thought, which he makes in terms of surface and depth: figures of speech are alterations of the material nature of language – changes to the shape or sound of a word; while figures of thought are alterations of their meaning – using one word to indicate something other than its literal definition. Quintilian's purpose in citing Cicero here is in fact to suggest that, as clear as the distinction seems to be between figures of speech and thought, there are certain figures that cannot be easily categorized. While Cicero allows for this possibility, Quintilian comments on it, and his comments are worth noting at length:

Some have held that there is only one Genus of Figures, though they have taken various views even of this: some, on the ground that any change of words entailed also a change of sense, have said that all Figures were a matter of words; others, on the ground that words were adapted to things, have said that they were all a matter of sense. Both of these views are obvious sophistries: for (1) the same things are often said in different ways and the sense stays the same though the expression has been changed, and (2) a Figure of Thought can contain several Figures of Speech, because the former resides in the conception and the latter in the presentation of the thought ... . Most writers in fact, so far as I know, have agreed that there are two classes of Figure: those of ... thought or mind or ideas ... and those of ... diction or Elocution or speech or style (*Institutio Oratoria* 9.1.15-17).

For Quintilian, the notion that figures of speech and thought can intersect is not just a remote possibility; it is a certainty. 'There are some Figures of Speech which are only slight modifications of Figures of Thought, for example Hesitation. ... The same principle applies to Correction. For what one doubts in the former Figure one corrects in this' (9.3.88). Hesitation and correction, he points out, are two figures that can be classified as both figures of speech and figures of thought. In this Quintilian does more than provide examples of Cicero's model. Instead, he sets up Cicero's model as one that is infinitely adaptable to future circumstances. For he shows that Cicero's insistence that a connection between surface and depth is central to rhetoric must be susceptible to cultural redefinition. What exactly will enable rhetoric to link language and the good will change with the times. But what his particular example shows us is something much more significant: his identification of hesitation and correction suggests that the crossover figures are ones that speak directly to issues of his era; it is for this reason that they are incapable of easy categorization.

Hesitation and correction

'Don't think you will scare me with words, son of Peleus, as if I were a little child. I can use taunts and abuse quite well if I like.

We know each other's lineage, we know the names of fathers, household tales among the children of men; but you have never set eyes on my parents, nor I on yours. Men say the admirable Peleus is your father, and your mother is Thetis the lovely daughter of the sea; for myself, I am proud to be the son of noble Anchises, and my mother is Aphrodite. One of those two houses will mourn a son this day; for I tell you, childish words will not be enough to part us.

'But if you care to know more of my lineage, that is no secret. First, Zeus Cloudgatherer had a son, Dardanos. He founded Dardania, and lived on the slopes of Ida among the running brooks, for sacred Ilios was not yet built upon the plain, and there was no city as yet … .

'Now let us stand no more talking like children in the space between the armies. We could load one another with curses enough to sink a ship as big as a mountain! The tongue of man runs on, with tales of all sorts in stock, and an infinite crop of words growing all round. Whatever kind of words you speak, such you will hear. But why must we bandy curses like a couple of scolding wives, who have some spite gnawing at their hearts until they run out and scold in the middle of the street, true and false together – the spite brings that in too! Your words will not turn me away from deeds when I mean battle. Come along now quickly, let us each taste what our mettle is like.'[19]

So speaks the Trojan Aeneas to the Greek Achilles. A minor moment in the *Iliad*, this speech of Aeneas, it can be argued, creates both the possibility and the context for the great Roman epic of the *Aeneid*. In this space of time and place on the battlefield, the space between the advancing armies, Aeneas lays out to Achilles and to the later readers of the epics the basis for his own (future) poem. His speech is brought on by taunting comments from Achilles that result in Aeneas' recounting his genealogy; Aeneas' genealogy forms the basis for the plot of the *Aeneid*, where Aeneas, having lost to the Greeks at Troy, travels west to found a new home in the land left by his forebear

Dardanus. Rome's founding is thus justified by the fact that Aeneas' ancestors once lived nearby; the development of the Roman empire is likewise justified by the journey Aeneas takes in getting back home.

In this speech as well, Aeneas also articulates for us the difference between the importance granted speech in the Greek archaic and Roman imperial worlds. In the *Iliad* Aeneas slots in his story, contrasting it to the action of the Greek world and denigrating it as the speech of women. By the time Aeneas' own story was told by Vergil, in the first century BCE, that space on the battlefield had become the rule rather than the exception, and the priorities Aeneas argues for here had become reversed. The place for battle, in the Roman world, occurs in the space between speeches.

This scene in the *Iliad*, then, can be seen not only as generative of the later Roman epic but also as indicative of the relative power granted speech in the empire. More than that, however, it offers to the Roman world an association between argument and delay: the delay in battle here creates the space for argument. Quintilian, we have seen, isolates delay, along with correction, as figures keyed into the Roman aesthetic; it can be argued that not only does the *Aeneid* derive from this space on the battlefield, but that Roman values overall, which often prioritize rhetoric over action, benefit from just such a delay.

To start with, of course, we need look no further than Quintilian himself, whose first major action in passing on the rhetorical system was one of both hesitation and correction – hesitation in his desire to conserve what Cicero had created, and correction when he felt he needed to bring him up to date. In the context of figures themselves Quintilian writes:

Anyone who wishes to acquire a broader grasp of these patterns of words and thoughts thus has a model to follow [in Cicero], and I do not think he could have better. But let him read what I have to say in the light of my own purpose (*Institutio Oratoria* 9.2.1).

Quintilian here pauses before the image of Cicero, urging the student to read his works on figures first. But he does so with a caveat: read those works alongside my own commentary on them; return to the works of the earlier master, but also be aware of the corrections Quintilian has suggested. Hesitation and correction, then, are, first and foremost, key tropes for understanding how Quintilian is reading and treating Cicero. As the *res publica* becomes adapted, manipulated, transformed into the empire, that body too is supplemented by other turns and transformations. The private acts of sitting down and looking back are the figures and turns in the literal fabric of empire, the acts of resistance that speak against the univocal propaganda. So, too, those gestures that cannot be classified – hesitation and correction – speak to an aesthetic of resistance and redefinition, whether it be political or, as in Quintilian's case, territorial.

In this way, these figures indicate their importance. Not only are Tiberius' understanding and presentation of Augustus – and Quintilian's of Cicero – arguably a conservative attempt to present his predecessor in a certain light, but throughout the literature of the empire this combination of conservatism and correction can be shown to be a prevailing aesthetic choice. What if the overriding authoritarianism of the time was in fact being reflected in an aesthetic of minor adjustment? To argue this point I want to offer two examples from Vergil and Ovid.

By the time Ovid wrote the *Metamorphoses*, delay – *mora* – had already acquired a certain thematic resonance. As Martha Malamud has eloquently argued, *mora* is central to the *Aeneid*. Some form of *mora* or *morari* occurs 63 times in the poem,[20] and delay serves as 'a structuring principle in the *Aeneid*. The first four books are structured around delay'. In addition, Jamie Masters[21] has argued that delaying strategies used by the narrator in Lucan's *Bellum Civile* play a key role, and David Quint, more broadly, has looked at relationships between gestures of resistance within the text and narrative form in *Epic and Empire*.[22] Malamud sums this up with the observation that 'the reluctance to speak the unspeakable' is a central characteristic of the '*Aeneid* and much of later Roman epic as well'.

Malamud's claim is supported by the use of hesitation in Vergil's *Aeneid*. Michael Putnam, and now Theodore Ziolkowski,[23] as part of a larger study, have examined Vergil's use of *cunctator/ cunctans*, the theme of hesitation throughout the *Aeneid*. Putnam has shown how the word occurs at critical moments – when Aeneas tries to seize the golden bough, when Turnus embarks on his final battle; most notoriously, when Aeneas himself prepares to sacrifice Turnus at the end of the poem ('at the one hesitating, Aeneas brandishes his fatal weapon': *cunctanti telum Aeneas fatale coruscat* [*Aeneid* 12.919]). In each of these instances, hesitation speaks against the grain of the imperial mission the poem on some level sets out to endorse. Hesitating, reflecting, pausing, reconsidering are all themes Vergil introduces to urge the reader to reconsider as well. The text stops at these moments, and while nothing can serve finally to undo the imperial mission the poem has embarked upon, it nonetheless sends a signal that this mission was not carried out without some level of defiance and consideration. Even as the conceit of looking back serves as a general trope for figures, so hesitation causes a work to stop, creating both a break in the surface level of the text and, more significantly, a fracture in the meaning as well.

For Quintilian to isolate hesitation as one of a very few acts that are difficult to categorize is thus an interesting move, suggesting that it is a figure that has more depth than might at first be apparent.

Mora/Amor/Roma

Nowhere does resistance find a greater spokesperson than in Ovid, and nowhere does the word *mora* occur with more frequency. The word appears throughout Ovid's oeuvre and recurs with great regularity in the *Metamorphoses*. It is in this context then that we should look at the story that Ovid tells about the word itself in the tale of Pyramus and Thisbe.

The story of Pyramus and Thisbe is known to the western tradition through its adaptation by Shakespeare as both the main plot of *Romeo and Juliet* and one of the subplots of *A Midsummer Night's Dream*, where the rude mechanicals rehearse and perform their version of Ovid's tale. Pyramus and Thisbe are star-crossed lovers whose proximity – they are neighbours – only heightens their frustration: their families are antagonists, and the wall between their houses both reifies and reinforces their enmity. Delay structures this story, from its beginning to its tragic end, as the lovers are kept from seeing one another and then, surmounting that obstacle and agreeing to meet by Ninus' tomb, they fail to intersect, causing the death of both, separately. The Ovidian innovation involves the transformation of the fruit of the tree that marks the place of their death – the mulberries, or *mora* – from white to red. This monument to delay stands perennially at the site of the lovers' demise. In so doing, it stands as a monument to delay in the context of love: the passage describing the transformation begins and ends with the two nouns that are identical except in the length of their first vowel, emphasizing the play on meanings (*Metamorphoses* 4.120-7):

> nec *mora*, ferventi moriens e vulnere traxit.
> ut iacuit resupinus humo, cruor emicat alte,
> non aliter quam cum vitiato fistula plumbo
> scinditur et tenui stridente foramine longas
> eiaculatur aquas atque ictibus aera rumpit.
> arborei fetus adspergine caedis in atram
> vertuntur faciem, madefactaque sanguine radix
> purpureo tinguit pendentia *mora* colore.[24]

It would be fair to say that all of Ovid's stories are about Rome, even as all of the *Aeneid* is ultimately about the founding of the Roman empire, one way or another. Ovid is even more explicit than Vergil in that he will remind the reader frequently of how other times and cultures are just like present-day Rome: even Olympus is said to be just like the Palatine Hill. One of the strangest details Ovid includes in the Pyramus and Thisbe story has a similar effect

of drawing the story forward to the present day: after Pyramus
stabs himself, the spurting wound is likened to a broken pipe
(*Metamorphoses* 4.122-4):

> just as when a waterpipe whose lead is weak bursts and shoots
> forth plumes of water from the slender, hissing gap, cutting the
> air with its spurts.

This form of plumbing is clearly more a detail from Ovid's Rome
than archaic Mesopotamia; its inclusion here urges us to see the
story as transpiring in the Rome of Ovid's time. 'Mora' stands as a
monument to delay in the context of Rome, and, in this, completes
the triad of anagrams offered by the city itself, as *mora*, together
with *amor*, mark the nature of *Roma*.

Moreover, the story's focus on haste and delay calls up a rich
subtext that draws the story even more clearly into the fabric of
Rome. As T.P. Wiseman has argued, the Romulus and Remus story,
repressed in much of the official literature, is a story on one level
about haste and delay. Wiseman writes:

> We are told that [Remus]' name derives from *remores*, a noun
> clearly related to the verb *remorari*, 'to delay'. ... Romulus'
> name connotes strength and vigour, but it is interpreted in a
> pejorative sense: hastiness and thoughtless action are what the
> various narrators of the foundation story associate with
> Romulus. ... Ovid [in the *Fasti*] characteristically plays with the
> theme in his account of Remus' death: Remus himself was *male
> velox* in leaping over the trench, and met his death at the 'hasty
> hand' (*temeraria manus*) of the aptly-named Celer [swift].[25]

Rome's foundation myth is thus not only a story about a dispute
between close families, but also a dispute that revolves around the
polarities of haste and delay. While the official version of this story
ended with Romulus – haste – winning and founding Rome, effectively erasing the story of Remus, Ovid's story ends with the

reification of delay in the mulberries (*mora*). Over this Ovid has laid a love story drawn from the elegiac tradition – an illicit affair where communication happens only surreptitiously. As Paul Allen Miller has recently shown, the elegiac tradition serves to articulate those things that are not presentable in epic;[26] Ovid, of course, has shown himself to be a pastmaster in undermining imperial goals in the dynamics of elegy. To juxtapose the suppressed foundation myth of Rome with the foundation story of elegy is to create a new foundation myth altogether. Pyramus and Thisbe is not just the story of star-crossed lovers; it is the story of what characterizes Rome in Ovid's mind: a collocation of stories that cannot be – or at least have not been – told. Where Ovid suggested in his elegies that Rome would be more accurately called Amor, in his later epic he suggests it would be better named Mora. The mulberries that turn from white to red not only call up the elegiac motif of the colour of the blushing skin of the beloved, they also suggest the prevalence of unspoken violence in the true story of Rome, one that is rooted in the stories of both *amor* and *mora*, love and delay.

Correction

In books 3 and 5 of the *Aeneid*, Vergil uses the geographic placement of the island of Sicily to make his strongest statement about empire. As Helenus informs us, the island was once connected to the mainland and broken off during repeated storms (*Aeneid* 3.414-19).

> These places, they say, at one time, wrenched by strength and widespread destruction (the passage of time enables such change), split apart – when first both lands were one, the sea broke through the middle and with the waves cut Italy's western shore from the Sicilian side, and washed the fields and separated towns on their shores with a narrow tide.

When Aeneas reaches Sicily later in book 3, Vergil goes to great lengths to emphasize that he does not sail through the divide between the two landmasses but, instead, sails around the island, thus in essence reconnecting the two lands, while insisting all the while on the separation. Given that Sicily was, according to Cicero (in *Verrines* 2.2.1), the province that made empire seem appealing, Vergil's choice cannot be unintentional. Jason, after all, and Odysseus had each sailed through the straits, despite the danger. Only Aeneas sails around. There is a further polemical level here: in the critical battle with Sextus Pompey in 42 BCE, Octavian, having lost, insisted on sailing around the island to reach Brundisium, even though he was already stationed at Rhegium. For Aeneas, then, to sail around rather than through the straits is for Vergil to make a proleptic strike for the importance of Sicily to the empire and its critical relationship with the mainland of Italy. Embracing Sicily serves as precursor to Octavian's eventual defeat of Sextus even as it offers a model for the imperial enterprise the epic is presuming. Aeneas' treatment of Sicily is a thoroughly political, polemical and imperial statement.

Yet, in Ovid's hands, this entire statement is undercut by the one simple act of sending Aeneas through the straits (*Metamorphoses* 14.75-7):

When the Trojan ships had successfully passed this [Scylla] and eager Charybdis, when they had already approached close to the Italian shore, they were borne back to the Libyan coast by a wind.

All the build-up, all the development Vergil gives to the importance of Sicily on the figurative level of his epic is undone by the one simple move of having Aeneas sail through the straits. This statement, of course, is reinforced in other ways throughout the *Metamorphoses*, most notably in the context of Sicily through Ovid's inclusion of the story of Arethusa as a model of empire as rape. Ovid is much less subtle in his anti-imperial statements than is Vergil. Yet the simplest move is in some ways the strongest: by correcting Aeneas' journey Ovid undercuts the imperialistic strain in Vergil's text.

Ovid's interest in hesitation and correction can be found throughout the *Metamorphoses*, yet there is one story in which he sets himself apart from the rest of the epic tradition, and he does so through a combination of hesitation and correction. At the beginning of the thirteenth book, when he has finally surpassed Vergil's twelve-book *Aeneid* in length, Ovid starts his own 'little *Aeneid*', telling the story of Aeneas and the aftermath of the fall of Troy. Stephen Hinds has vividly described how this moment for Ovid is a turning point in his epic;[27] in this discussion Hinds comments on the 'gotcha' aspect of Ovid starting in the thirteenth book where Vergil had left off in the twelfth, and he describes beautifully how Ovid's *Aeneid* differs from Vergil's. Hinds' observation that Ovid's choice to write his *Aeneid* starting in the thirteenth book should be seen as a riposte to Vergil is surely right. What I wish to focus on here, though, is the actual story that begins the thirteenth book, the one that both precedes and prepares for his telling of the Aeneas story.

Ovid begins the thirteenth book of the *Metamorphoses* with the debate between Ajax and Odysseus over Achilles' armour. This is the only true debate in the *Metamorphoses*, and it has attracted the attention of many readers looking for rhetoric in Ovid. Yet this debate is significant for its placement as well as its style: it is my contention that Ovid places the debate here as an introduction to his little *Aeneid*, and that he intends the reader to see it not only as a rehearsal of the story made famous in Homer's *Odyssey* and elsewhere but also, on an allegorical level, as Ovid's way of asserting his rights to the Vergilian material. The debate between Ajax and Odysseus, in other words, is also a debate between Vergil and Ovid in which Ovid, as the more verbally agile of the two, wins, and Vergil, bested in this contest, not only loses but dies, thus becoming effectively silenced. If read this way, the debate between Ajax and Odysseus stands as a prime example of correction: even as Odysseus corrects Ajax's version of the truth, so Ovid asserts that his version is truer, both of this tale and of the *Aeneid* material that follows.

On the one hand, we have Ajax, known for his strength on the battlefield; on the other, Ulysses, known for his verbal artistry. The subject of the debate is the distribution of Achilles' armour following his death. Ajax speaks first, and in a short speech of only a hundred or so lines argues for his right to the arms primarily on the basis of his physical prowess and his blood relationship with Achilles. He puts Ulysses down as a coward who uses deception to cover his failures. Ulysses then responds, arguing at much greater length and using more obvious rhetorical devices: he draws on many of the tools Cicero recommends, including rhetorical questions, verbal artistry (repetition, puns, etc.) and gestures, even baring his chest at the end to show the wounds he acquired in battle. He answers each of Ajax's points one by one, then moves on to show how, in addition to winning each of those points, he has other things to recommend him as the victor: most notably his tactical skill, which makes him not only critical *to* any battle but also prominent *before*, thus granting him precedence over 'mere' fighters such as Ajax. He argues this last point several different ways and at different times, in each asserting that anything Ajax claims actually belongs to Ulysses, since victory in battle is as much a matter of strategy as it is of strength.

To a large extent, the surprising character here is Ajax. Literary history, by Ovid's time, offers us two very different versions of the outcome of the debate. On the one hand, we have the Ajax of the *Odyssey*, who refuses to speak to Odysseus when he encounters him in the underworld, precisely because of the outcome of this very debate. On the other, we have Vergil's adaptation of this story, in the encounter between Dido and Aeneas in the underworld: in this instance it is Dido who plays the part of Ajax, remaining mute before the pleading Aeneas ostensibly because of anger over his abandonment of her. Even though Ovid's tale is based literally on the first, it is heavily shaded by the second: we cannot, I would submit, encounter the Ajax of the debate in the *Metamorphoses* without having both of these images in our mind and, as a result, we are struck by two things at once: we see Ajax through the Vergilian gloss of Dido, and that adaptation of Ajax has had a devastating effect on the Iliadic hero: rather than being impressed by his speech, we hear it – and Ovid encourages us in this – as Dido's lament over Aeneas; we hear, that is, Ajax not as the Homeric Ajax, but as Dido, for here we have an Ajax debating a much more focused speaker, even as Dido debates the departing Aeneas in *Aeneid* 4. This Ajax, then, is also the Dido of books 4 and 6 of the *Aeneid*. He is doomed from the start.

This sense of doom is carried over into his speech, where Ajax makes it clear that it is Ulysses who is the orator; he is just the fighter. The fact that his speech is well constructed cannot compete with the fact that the reader knows the outcome of the debate, and that Ajax foreshadows that outcome with his own sense of help-lessness, aided and abetted by the fact that we read him as a version of Dido.

Moreover, this Ajax is not just a Dido figure. He is also portrayed as Aeneas, both by Ovid and by Ulysses. The debate begins in a context that reminds the reader of the opening of the second book of the *Aeneid*: there, as here, the men are gathered, awaiting a speech. Even as Aeneas identifies himself often through his genealogy, so Ajax begins by attaching his line to that of Achilles. But perhaps most striking is the fact that, when Ulysses speaks, he describes Ajax as someone who could neither identify the features on the shield nor understand their import. Aeneas is described in just such terms as he shoulders his own shield at the end of *Aeneid* 8.

The identification of Ajax with both Dido and Aeneas suggests that Ovid is doing more than asking us to read him in a Vergilian context. By suggesting that Ajax is both Dido *and* Aeneas Ovid suggests, rather, that we should see this hero as a quintessentially Vergilian construct, and in that he broadens the scope to suggest that the debate is not only between Ajax and Ulysses, but between the quintessentially Vergilian hero and Ulysses, or between Vergil's sense of epic and another, earlier Homeric form. The first fact we learn about Ajax is that he already has a shield, a fact that Ulysses reminds us of later; if the shield is, as it would appear to be, the subject matter of epic, then the Vergilian hero already has his.

This lining up of characters is borne out by the end of Ajax's speech (*Metamorphoses* 13.120-2):

> 'denique (quid verbis opus est?) spectemur agendo!
> arma viri fortis medios mittantur in hostes:
> inde iubete peti et referentem ornate relatis.'

'At last (what is the need for words?) let us be seen in action. Let the arms of the brave man be sent into the midst of our enemy: then order them sought and equip the one bringing them back with them, having been brought back.'

The careful reader will see here two embedded references, especially if the Latin is consulted, for the second line begins 'arma viri', which is a clear allusion to the opening words of the *Aeneid*, 'arma virumque cano'. But more striking is that juxtaposed to the reference to the *Aeneid* is an equally potent reference to the passage from *Iliad* 20 with which we began this section, in which Aeneas argues with Achilles about the delay posed by argument. Ajax is not only an Aeneas character, he is, in Ovid's depiction, the ur-Aeneas, the Aeneas from both the *Iliad* and the *Aeneid*. In juxtaposing these two characters, Ovid succeeds in reintroducing the theme of hesitation in the context of correction.

All this succeeds in setting the stage for Ulysses. Ulysses' victory in the debate comes about in large part because he speaks after Ajax: he has material to respond to, which he does with finesse, and, having struck down all the arguments Ajax proposed, he adds his own material. Unlike Ajax, Ulysses is unencumbered by a Vergilian gloss. Vergil, responding himself to Homer, deliberately does not show Ulysses except in one small vignette in book 2. We bring no Vergilian baggage to our reading of Ovid's Ulysses. As a result, he is free to present himself in a non-Vergilian way, which is exactly what he does. The Ulysses Ovid depicts is a wonderful free, new, and Ovidian creation. Clever with words, he is also strikingly elegiac: when he confronts Ajax about his actions during the Trojan stalemate, he lists his own in a way that recalls predominant strategies – metaphor, voice, tone – from Ovid's own earlier elegies (*Metamorphoses* 13.212-15):

> quis tuus usus erat? nam si mea facta requiris,
> hostibus insidior, fossa munimina cingo,
> consolor socios ut longi taedia belli
> mente ferant placida, doceo quo simus alendi
> armandique modo, mittor quo postulat usus.

What need did you serve? If you ask what I did, I trapped the enemy; I circled the fortifications with a ditch; I sturdied our allies so that they could bear the tedium of long war with a calm heart; I taught how we were to be fed and armed; I was sent where need demanded.

Most striking of all are Ulysses' arguments about his pre-eminence. In telling the story of saving Ajax from retreat he argues, 'from that time on, whatever that one seems to have done that was brave is my doing, I who brought him, turning tail, back in' (*Metamorphoses* 13.238-40). But he also says this about another early hero, Achilles ('therefore his feats are mine' *ergo opera illius me sunt* [*Met*.13.173]), suggesting that his influence goes back beyond Ajax to Achilles himself. *Altaque posse capi faciendo Pergama cepi*: by enabling the capture of Troy he himself captured it. Ulysses as enabler, of hero and epic, is the characterization Ovid supplies.

Ulysses wins both because he speaks second and because he inscribes himself into the earlier narratives, thus claiming pre-eminence. This doubly powerful position is one that Ovid claims for himself throughout the *Metamorphoses*. By starting his poem not with the Trojan war but with the beginning of the cosmos, Ovid is able to suggest that he in fact precedes Vergil. He thus writes himself into Vergil's narrative even as he rewrites and corrects it. The story of Ajax and Ulysses describes the process of narrative correction even as it performs it: it provides us with an example of correction in both a subjective and an objective sense. Through correcting Ajax's version of the story, Ulysses ensures victory for himself; through this debate Ovid ensures victory for his little *Aeneid* both in terms of actual rewriting of Vergilian characters of Dido and Aeneas as the losing Ajax and through the parable of inscription the tale provides. By the time the debate is finished, Ovid has proclaimed himself ready to write the story of the *Aeneid* on his own terms. We await with excitement the way in which this tale will be retold and the ways that will cause us to rethink Vergil's own epic.

But of course the same argument can be made about the passage from the *Iliad* with which we began this section. In the context of the Homeric poem, rhetoric comes second to action; once Aeneas becomes a hero in his own right, all of his statements in the *Iliad* take on an ironic tinge, as the beginning of the passage quoted above runs through the very heritage of Aeneas that justifies the Trojans settling in Italy and suggests that Aeneas's story both predates and outlasts that of Achilles. The *Aeneid* not only derives from the delay in battle in *Iliad* 20, its plot can be seen as a direct correction of that scene. Like Ulysses in the Ovidian debate with Ajax, Vergil corrects Homer by stalling the plot.

Conclusion

Quintilian identifies the tropes of correction and hesitation as not easy to categorize and so suggests that, like repetition in contemporary society, those figures are key to the aesthetic of the culture. Looking back at representative examples of these tropes in Vergil and Ovid reveals how each serves to carve out a space for a Roman aesthetic, starting with a reworking of the relative value of speech and action in the inherited tradition of Greek literature. But hesitation and correction also serve to create a space for Roman community, one that draws those who read Latin together in response to the Greek tradition that comes before. In the space on the battlefield – which becomes the space of the forum or the courtroom – Roman rhetoric prevails. The figures of hesitation and correction identify the marks that characterize areas of importance in Roman texts.

3

Dwelling on a Point: Rhetoric and Love in the Middle Ages

In the Middle Ages the story of figures becomes a story of love. The adaptation of the classical system of rhetoric depends in large part on the play of love that permeates medieval discourse, both in terms of the subjects discussed in many of the poems and stories, and also in terms of the process of communication. Love can be seen as responsible for enabling the adaptation of the classical modes of rhetoric into forms that are both useful and representative of medieval culture, even as rhetoric came to enable language to participate in the power of love. In particular, Augustine's understanding of selfless love, or *caritas*, in the *De Doctrina Christiana* and elsewhere, as the motion of the soul toward God, is rooted in a Neoplatonic understanding of love as a generative force and so links love with motion. But when rhetoric became adapted, in the high Middle Ages, to a renewed interest in the world, love too was adapted to fit these needs. The topic of courtly love that prevails in vernacular literature of the twelfth and thirteenth centuries can be shown to have its roots in the rhetorical tradition; so, too, the intersection of love and language that Augustine posits in the *De Doctrina Christiana* continues to inform rhetorical discussions, even after love comes to mean something quite different from *caritas*.

Treatises on figures

In the medieval treatises on poetry, figures remained a consistent and essential element of the rhetorical tradition. The system of figures was transmitted intact, and even when the application of rhetoric moved from the forum and the education of the young man to its triple appearance in the arts of letter writing, preaching, and poetry, we find that it is rhetoric's flexibility and resourcefulness that remained, enabling it to survive such fragmentation.[1] Rhetoric became a school topic, one of the trivium of liberal arts, joining dialectic and grammar, and would seem to have escaped from its initial setting, detached, as Vickers argues, from its social and political context.[2] But it is the continuities from Cicero and Quintilian into the high Middle Ages that should be emphasized: despite the fracturing created by manuscript transmission and change in milieu, an aspect – a critical aspect, as we have seen – of the rhetorical corpus is carried through, that of the importance of figures. This emphasis on figures can be seen as a shift from 'subject matters' to 'verbal forms';[3] as we shall see, however, it becomes a means to the embrace of the world that surrounds the speaker and so an adaptation of rhetoric to the questions and pressures of this world.

By the high Middle Ages, rhetoric had become something very different from the art practised by Cicero or Quintilian. As a discipline associated strongly with the pagan past, figurative language was resisted in the Christian Middle Ages, denigrated as an art of style more than substance, a practice of the flesh more than of the spirit. As Miller, Prosser, and Benson argue,[4] only those classical works 'baptized' by Augustine in *De Doctrina Christiana* (c. 395/6) escape the criticism levelled against rhetoric. This 'baptism' affects the rhetorical discipline as well: the *De Doctrina*, especially its fourth book on style (which, together with a part of the third book, was added in c. 426/7, possibly from notes from an earlier draft) transformed rhetoric by presenting it as an art of interpretation, rather than persuasion, that was dependent on the pursuit of Christian truth. Yet the seeds for this were already planted in Quintilian, in whose work, as we have seen, the importance of reading the canon critically was introduced into the discipline. Even as the image of the author shifted in late antiquity from a classical model, based largely on Vergil, to a scriptural model in which the author is a scribe of the truth,[5] so rhetoric was transformed during late antiquity and the early Middle Ages from a civic tool to a hermeneutic one, capable of offering an approach acceptable for both sacred and secular works. Taught in the schools as part of the liberal arts curriculum, rhetoric was offered first as a means of confronting and accommodating extant texts.

Moreover, love enters into the equation through Augustine's understanding of the interpretive process. In the *De Doctrina Christiana* Augustine asserts, famously, that texts can be read with either of two kinds of love, charity or cupidity, the first being an interpretation that offers a reading that points toward God and Christian truth, the second, a reading that draws away from God towards the transient things of this world. While love was also a part of the rhetorical process in the writings of Plato, it becomes associated in Augustine's hands with the difference between the eternal and the transitory, between the invisible and the visible, the immaterial and the material.

In this context, figures pose problems. The decoration of speech was perceived as associated with interests that would lead away from the higher truth towards the fleshly concerns of this world. In the high Middle Ages, however, figures resurface as essential. As Rita Copeland has noted, in the field of the *ars poetica*, or rhetorical poetics, of the high Middle Ages, we witness the legacy of Augustine's synthesis of rhetoric and hermeneutics: 'as in Augustine's program, [these treatises] define rhetorical *inventio* through exegetical procedure'.[6] These treatises, which teach how to approach a topic, are also the legacy of the sections on figures of speech and thought from the Ciceronian tradition; it is, then, in these tracts that we see most clearly the adaptation of the classical tradition by the Christian medieval world. And through their use of figures – the 'flowers of rhetoric' – we can watch how tropes progress from representing a world that is composed of material distractions to one in which those very same objects provide the means for achieving spiritual insight. The space carved out by hesitation and correction in ancient texts becomes, in works of the high Middle Ages, a literal, architectural space in the text that enables the flourishing of understanding. But more than this, figures create the architecture that enables love to thrive because love, through Augustine in particular, becomes linked with language and interpretation.

Anomalies in the treatises

Medieval works on figures are derived, as Edmond Faral has clearly demonstrated, from the treatise on style, *Ad Herennium,* attributed to Cicero. In Faral's book *Les Arts poétiques du 12me et du 13me siècle,* which gathers together a collection of important Latin treatises from the twelfth and thirteenth centuries on how to compose poetry, the *Ad Herennium* is clearly the most important ancient source.[7] While the ancient treatise covers all five faculties of rhetoric from invention to delivery, and the necessary parts of a discourse, from the introduction to the conclusion, it is the fourth book, which discusses only style, that was copied and studied throughout the Middle Ages. Within this book, after covering the three kinds of style, grand, middle, and simple, and the qualities appropriate to each, the treatise moves to a discussion of figures of speech and figures of thought, which it distinguishes in terms of manipulation of language versus manipulation of ideas.

Turning to Faral's useful chart of medieval treatises drawn from the *Ad Herennium,*[8] one finds that the same figures were borrowed wholesale, with new examples provided, by key treatises of the twelfth and thirteenth centuries. While the order of the figures may change radically – as in the treatise of Saint-Omer – the names of the figures are remarkably consistent, thus making it possible for Faral to trace the source to the *Ad Herennium.* In Geoffrey of Vinsauf's treatise, the *Poetria Nova,* there is one figure that is noticeable by its omission and whose absence is noted at the start: 'In this list, learn what are the tropes: how many (twice ten if you subtract one) and what order they hold'.[9] This seems an awkward way to state that there are nineteen figures of thought discussed, until the list is compared to that offered by the *Ad Herennium,* where there are indeed twenty.

Moreover, the one figure that is omitted in the *Poetria Nova* is one that, it turns out, the *Ad Herennium* refuses to exemplify because it was so embedded in the project as a whole, *commoratio*. At the start of the section of the *Ad Herennium* that covers figures, it is clearly stated that the purpose of the treatise is to provide new examples for each of the figures. While the focus of the debate that begins the fourth book is on whether the examples are to be drawn from the ancients or the moderns, the fact remains that the opening gambit of the book is its justification on the grounds of examples provided by the author himself. Given this, it is particularly striking that there is one figure for which the author refuses to provide even one example (*Ad Herennium* 4.45.58):

> *Commoratio*: occurs when one remains rather long upon, and often returns to, the strongest topic on which the whole cause rests. Its use is particularly advantageous, and is especially characteristic of the good orator, for no opportunity is given the hearer to remove his attention from this strongest topic. I have been unable to subjoin a quite appropriate example of the figure, because this topic is not isolated from the whole cause like some limb, but like blood is spread through the whole body of the discourse.[10]

Commoratio, or dwelling on a point, is the basis for all other figures as well as for the treatise as a whole, and thus is central to the collection of figures found in the fourth book of the *Ad Herennium*.

It is *commoratio* that Geoffrey signals, and he is not alone: from Matthew of Vendôme to Geoffrey of Vinsauf, John of Garland, and others, it is *commoratio*, understood broadly as amplification, that becomes the purpose and reason for deploying figures overall. Abbreviation, or the lack of amplification, becomes its defining negation. Through this, medieval rhetoric becomes focused on what the *Ad Herennium* describes as the lifeblood of the rhetorical work, the figure of *commoratio*; all other figures become subsumed under that heading and exemplify the one that cannot be separated out and defined. In the medieval treatises, *commoratio* falls out of the list of figures as it becomes the rubric for figures in general, which is, in turn, defined by its antithesis, *brevitas*.

A clear example of this adaptive process can be seen in the *Laborintus* of Evrard the German. Under the list of tropes we find the following summarizing sentence: 'This song is redolent of twice ten flowers: take away one: that one does not have a place'.[11] Again the one that is missing is *commoratio*, which, strikingly, heads the whole list: 'if long delay (*mora longa*) pleases, I am not friendly to abbreviation'. The reason to decorate a speech is to amplify it: the term for amplification, *mora*, is shorthand for *commoratio*, the figure that drops from the list, the figure that subsumes all figurative speech, according to the *Ad Herennium*.

From the *Ad Herennium* we learn that there is one term that is so embedded in the process of style that it cannot be exemplified. Because of this status it drops out of the list and becomes, instead, the rubric for all figurative speech: the organizing principle of the purpose of style. The fact that medieval treatises are organized around amplification and abbreviation suggests not only the preva-lence of the *Ad Herennium*, as Faral so clearly indicates, but also the centrality of *commoratio*, or dwelling on a point, to the high medieval mindset.

We need to ask what *commoratio* offers as the key trope. The *Ad Herennium*, in separating it out, opens the door to the centrality of dwelling on a point, as *commoratio* becomes subsumed or reinter-preted as amplification and, in turn, used as the central concept of figuration in the Middle Ages. What does *commoratio* offer the medieval author?

Commoratio

Commoratio is a form of amplification. In his early thirteenth-century treatise, *Documentum de arte versificandi*, Geoffrey of Vinsauf offers an interesting instance of amplification that echoes the descriptions of *commoratio*. Let us, he says, take the shortest

72

possible text, a single verb, and show how amplification works. The
example Geoffrey chooses is the verb *lego*, 'I read':

> This is the material proposed to us: I read (*lego*). First from this
> verb we may elicit three things: namely the person, the meaning
> of the verb, and the place. Thus, 'I am reading in such a place'.[12]

He continues:

> Whatever the verb is, whether transitive or absolute, there is in
> addition a third property, namely the time or place. From these
> two follow everything. For example: 'I read in such a place or at
> such a time' 'I play at such a time, such a place'.[13]

According to Geoffrey, a single verb entails a setting. In his example
of *lego*:

> This place contains in itself a double opportunity for study,
> partly from the joy of its beauty, and partly from its removal
> from the noise of the crowd. ... The occasion of this opportunity,
> since it is in harmony with the ease of those who study, invited
> me completely to study and found me eager for fruitful
> reading. ... For in the appropriate occasion of knowledge and
> frequent reading I blossom forth – when the wind blows more
> gently you will bloom with promised fruit.[14]

The beauty of the place, the harmony of silent reading in the
company of others, and the material being read are all elements
packed into the single verb, *lego*; revealing them forms part of the
process of amplification.

There is a striking parallel provided by the scene of Ambrose
reading silently in book 6 of Augustine's *Confessions*; one phrase in
particular links the scenes, and through this we can catch a glimpse
of how the role of rhetoric changed between Augustine's time and
that of Geoffrey. Augustine posits that Ambrose reads silently in an

effort to recharge his mind between debates with 'crowds of men with arbitrations to submit to him, to whose frailties he ministered'.

> Very often when we were there, we saw him silently reading and never otherwise. After sitting for a long time in silence (for who would dare to burden him in such intent concentration?) we used to go away. We supposed that in the brief time he could find for his mind's refreshment, free from the hubbub of other people's troubles, he would not want to be invited to consider another problem. We wondered if he read silently perhaps to protect himself in case he had a hearer interested and intent on the matter, to whom he might have to expound the text being read if it contained difficulties, or who might wish to debate some difficult questions.[15]

Escaping the hubbub provides the purpose of reading for both Ambrose and Geoffrey. Yet in Geoffrey's case, reading is the exemplar of rhetorical amplification: it is what rhetoric serves to do. For Ambrose, as presumably for Augustine, reading is opposed to the role of rhetoric, which is to debate the meaning of the text. Reading has little or nothing to do with rhetoric for Ambrose and everything to do with it for Geoffrey. It is a means to self-discovery for Geoffrey; a means to escape only for Ambrose. It is, I would argue, no accident that 'I read' is Geoffrey's example for amplification. Geoffrey will, at the end, confirm this, by adducing as a proverb suitable for concluding this rhetorical exercise: 'The solitude of the place is fitting for readers and for the withdrawn leisure of students, free from the approach of men and the noise of tongues. ... Sufficient proof of this is deduced from this place. The less it occupies itself, the more it occupies the student.' By the thirteenth century, the space of the forum in ancient Rome had been replaced by a space in which man achieves understanding. As Geoffrey explains:

> A proverb is used near the beginning in this way: 'Whose mind yearns for the heights of the highest achievement, completely

longs for the fruit and abundance of reading.' And, according to the previous doctrine, one must continue the material this way: 'And let this proof be witness to this thing, the one most desirous toward reading, the most fervent for achievement.'

An example of a proverb used near the middle: 'Perusal of books with frequent repetition is the correct way to profit in knowledge.' What the Ethics of Cato intimates sufficiently is the following paternal admonition: 'Read books.' It should be continued in this way: '… to profit in knowledge. This the Ethics of Cato intimates sufficiently. For I am taught these things by more familiar evidence.'[16]

Here is the crux of the argument: reading occurs at the intersection of text and world. It is the place where learning and living coincide. Life and letters come together in this rhetoric, in this reading. Amplification is indeed a *commoratio*, 'dwelling' as both noun and verb: rhetoric is the process of joining language to life, and life to language; amplification enables experience to unpack learning, even as learning enables us to comprehend our present situation.

Stephen Johnson's 2005 book, *Everything Bad is Good for You*,[17] provides a pertinent counterexample to Geoffrey's claims. While amplification, as we have been told repeatedly by the treatises of the twelfth and thirteenth centuries, was the dominant trope at that time, precisely, we have argued, because it enables the intersection of life and letters through reading, it is lost, or redefined, in the current atmosphere. In Johnson's book, video games and complex TV plots are credited with raising the average IQ because of the many demands they place on the observer. In a fictional, and avowedly ironic, speculation, Johnson imagines what might have been said about reading if it had come after the video revolution. Reading, he proposes, would have been seen to 'understimulate the senses' since it offers little more than 'a barren string of words on the page'. Moreover, books are 'tragically isolating', forcing the reader to 'sequester him or herself in a quiet space'. But what is perhaps most damaging is that books 'follow a fixed linear path. You can't control their narratives in any fashion – you simply sit back and have the story dictated to you. ... This risks instilling a general passivity. ... Reading is not an active, participatory process; it's a submissive one.'

We do not need to see this as merely hypothetical. Geoffrey of Vinsauf is describing exactly this – the moment when reading first became a general phenomenon and, to all intents and purposes, introduced precisely these issues: words on the page, isolation, sequestering in a quiet space; and from his description we can see the fatal flaw of Johnson's speculation: for narratives, created through amplification, are anything but linear, and the process of reading Geoffrey describes is anything but passive. His example of amplification is about reading, not writing: he presents reading as the ultimate hermeneutic exercise, precisely because it allows you to be sequestered from the hustle-bustle of the world and encourages you to reflect on the intersection of your experiences and those you read. It provides, in short, a place for the intersection of language and ethos as you bring your understanding to bear on the words you are reading: hardly passive or submissive.

In this, Geoffrey echoes the writings of Abbot Suger (1080/81-1151). Suger was primarily a churchman but also an admirable ambassador for both church and state. While a monk at Saint-Denis, Suger served both his king, Louis VI, and the abbot of Saint-Denis. When he became abbot himself, his renovations of the abbey, while prompted largely by practical needs, laid the foundation for what became the Gothic style. When Suger describes himself delighting in the renovated church of Saint-Denis, he does so in the following words (in the *De Administratione*):

unde, cum ex dilectione decoris domus Dei aliquando multi-color gemmarum speciositas ab exintrinsecis me curis devocaret, sanctarum etiam diversitatem virtutum, de materi-alibus ad immaterialia transferendo, honesta meditatio insistere persuaderet, videor videre me quasi sub aliqua extranea orbis terrarum plaga, quae nec tota sit in terrarum faece nec tota in coeli puritate, demorari, ab hac etiam inferiori

ad illam superiorem anagogico more Deo donante posse trans-
ferri.[18]

Thus when – out of my delight in the beauty of the house of God
– the loveliness of the many-colored gems has called me away
from external cares, and worthy meditation has induced me to
reflect, transferring that which is material to that which is
immaterial, on the diversity of the sacred virtues: then it seems
to me I see myself dwelling, as it were, in some strange region
of the universe which neither exists entirely in the slime of the
earth nor entirely in the purity of Heaven; and that, by the
grace of God, I can be transported from this inferior to that
higher world in an anagogical manner.

For Suger, the spiritual ecstasy he finds in the glorious stained
glass, jewels, and gold that cover the interior of his church is a place
from which he can reach out, and up, to find God. The beauty is an
essential step to the truth; yet more important, it would seem, is the
place and act of dwelling, *demorari*. Communing with the beauty of
the renovated church, Suger articulates a process similar to that of
reading as described by Geoffrey of Vinsauf. Both Geoffrey and
Suger describe an intimate space in which the self can be transported to 'some strange region of the universe which neither exists
entirely in the slime of the earth nor entirely in the purity of
heaven'. The space of the forum has been transferred to the space of
understanding.
   What this passage asks us to focus on is the here and now of
Suger's surroundings because they evoke ascension, to use a term
from his favourite philosophers, pseudo-Dionysius the Areopagite
and John Scotus, who describe the ascent from the material to the
immaterial as the anagogical or upward-leading method. The essence
of Suger's spiritual existence lies in the material wealth that
surrounds him. Dwelling as both noun and verb – the place and the
action of lingering – are linked both with place and with the anagogical method.

Love and space

Suger's works deserve further discussion in this context, since his efforts that led to the beauty described above are equally rhetorical even as they shed light on the meaning and understanding of the concept of 'dwelling'. Under Suger's watchful gaze, the abbey church of Saint-Denis was transformed from a dark, close abbey into a lofty structure filled with light and colour, now heralded as the first Gothic cathedral. His accomplishments are all the more astonishing when set in their historical context: the powerful force of Saint Bernard of Clairvaux and the stark aesthetic of the Cistercian order constantly questioned Suger's choices and decisions. It is to defend these moves, in large part, that Suger writes his autobiographical *De Administratione*; his defence is found as well in the numerous letters and charters that have been preserved.

Suger is not a rhetorician. Nonetheless, it is clear that the works he writes describing and justifying his renovations to the abbey of Saint-Denis are informed by a clear knowledge of the rhetorical tradition. In particular, he uses, as we shall see, rhetorical arguments about expansion to justify his renovations. Yet rhetoric is not 'just' a linguistic tool for him; it clearly informs his view of history and the world, and his understanding of amplification entails a concept that is both literal and metaphoric. The association of physical renovation with rhetorical terms speaks to a redefinition of rhetoric as a system capable of capturing the intersection of public and private perception.

Abbot Suger's decision to renovate is presented most succinctly in the *Chartes*:

nono decimo administrationis nostrae anno, cum novo operi in anteriori ecclesiae parte libenter et fideliter desudassemus ... subito sanctorum Martyrum dominorum et protectorum nostrorum amor et devotio nos ad augmentandam et amplificandam superioris ecclesiae partem capitalem rapuit.[19]

3. Dwelling on a Point

In the nineteenth year of our administration, after we had applied ourselves willingly and faithfully to the front part of the church with the new construction, ... the love and devotion for our holy Martyrs, lords and protectors, suddenly drove our chapter to augment and amplify part of the upper church.

Having reworked the front of the church, Suger states, he turned his attention to the chapel at the back. The questions that plague much of the rest of his writings – of the need or desire for luxury, of the importance of light and beauty, of the centrality of the visible and material to the finished work – are not even hinted at here. With one part completed, Suger turned to the other.

Suger provides his fullest rationalization for the expansion in the *De Consecratione*:

When the glorious and famous King of the Franks, Dagobert, notable for his royal magnanimity in the administration of his kingdom and yet no less devoted to the Church of God, had fled to the village of Catulliacum in order to evade the intolerable wrath of his father Clothaire the Great, and when he had learned that the venerable images of the Holy Martyrs who rested there – appearing to him as very beautiful men clad in snow-white garments – requested his service and unhesitatingly promised him their aid with words and deeds, he decreed with admirable affection that a basilica of the Saints be built with regal magnificence. When he had constructed this [basilica] with a marvelous variety of marble columns he enriched it incalculably with treasures of purest gold and silver and hung on its walls, columns and arches tapestries woven of gold and richly adorned with a variety of pearls, so that it might seem to excel the ornaments of all other churches and, blooming with incomparable luster and adorned with every terrestrial beauty, might shine with inestimable splendor. Only one thing was wanting in him: that he did not allow for the size that was necessary. Not that anything was lacking in his devotion or good will; but perhaps there existed thus far, at that time of the Early Church, no [church] either greater or [even] equal in size; or perhaps [he thought that] a smallish one – reflecting the splendor of gleaming gold and gems to the admiring eyes more keenly and delightfully because they were nearer – would glow with greater radiance than if it were built larger.

Through a fortunate circumstance attending this singular smallness [*brevitatis*] – the number of the faithful growing and frequently gathering to seek the intercession of the Saints – the aforesaid basilica had come to suffer grave inconveniences. Often on feast days, completely filled, it disgorged through all its doors the excess of the crowds as they moved in opposite directions, and the outward pressure of the foremost ones not only prevented those attempting to enter from entering but also expelled those who had already entered (*De Consecratione* 2).[20]

Suger's professed interest lies in redeeming the building from its *brevitas* by enlarging it (*amplificandam*). The use of *brevitas* to describe narrowness is striking: one would expect instead a spatial term like *angustia*.[21] Contemporary rhetorical treatises attest that *brevitas* and *amplificatio* are rhetorical, not architectural, terms. Moreover, *brevitas* is a term that becomes increasingly associated with novelty and modernity, as wordiness and imitation are argued to be the habits of the ancients. Suger's insistence that he needs to rescue the church from its *brevitas* through amplification is a subtle, yet brilliant, adaptation of these rhetorical terms. Not only does he project rhetorical categories onto the world, he asserts as well that his radical decisions to renovate the abbey, for which he receives criticism, especially from Bernard of Clairvaux, are the most conservative of actions: he is, after all, engaged in amplification, not brevity: he is on the side of promoting tradition, not novelty. Suger's justifications for his renovations are a testimony to the importance of amplification to the culture.

Amplification, though, is here rooted in the real: through his renovations, Suger not only beautified the church but also expanded it drastically and, in so doing, created a space for worship and meditation. At first this would seem to run counter to the notion of love associated with rhetoric in Augustine's seminal text, but Augustine spells out his understanding of *caritas* in another text that is then expanded upon by Hugh of Saint Victor. Augustine distinguishes between the same two types of love in the following terms (*Enarratio in Psalmum* 9:15, *Patrologia Latina* 36, col.124a):

> pes animae recte intelligitur amor; qui cum pravus, vocatur *cupiditas* aut libido: cum autem rectus, dilectio vel *caritas* ... ad ambulandum et proficiendum et ascendendum *caritas* movet; ad cadendum superbia movet.

> The foot of the soul is rightly understood as love which, when depraved, is called cupidity or lust, when righteous, love or charity. ... Charity moves through walking, advancing and climbing; pride moves to a fall.

Augustine makes it clear, in the lines that follow, that he is talking about a spiritual 'foot'. Yet in phrasing the opposition between *caritas* and *cupiditas* in this way, he offers a new understanding and treatment of the terms. In his commentary on the Divine Hierarchies of pseudo-Dionysius the Areopagite, Hugh of Saint Victor talks about love in a way that both resonates with the passage in Augustine even as it clarifies love in a new light (*PL* 175, col. 1037b):

> And what of love? ... Where love is, there is drive and heat, or rather, where is love without heat and drive? They who were walking and loving, burning and driving, why did they speak about Jesus, whom they heard and did not recognize on the road? They were walking and they were moved, driven by the impatience of love, since if they stood still they would not love.

The motion of love that lies at the heart of Augustine's statements about *caritas* and that he intends to be understood as a spiritual, allegorical, upward-heading movement is here, by Hugh of Saint Victor, construed in a linear, literal fashion. Love, he says, involves not only spiritual but pedestrian motion.

Later in the same treatise Hugh writes that love is both a force in motion and an entity that needs room to move. Moreover, the space it requires is of a particular sort:

> and [love] reaches your innermost heart, then it enters into you and you also enter so that it can either remain or squat outside yourself, either on your doorstep, or in your courtyard or before the door of your house, … [let him] come all the way to your bed, and let him enter your bedroom, and penetrate all the way to the innermost sanctum and let him rest in your intimacy.

What we are offered here is a very different understanding of love from that normally associated with Augustinian *caritas*. Marked by motion and physical presence, as well as by space, love is not an escape from the material, but an embrace of it.

Abbot Suger draws on these passages to justify his expansion of the abbey church of Saint-Denis. Suger frames his argument in physical – architectural – terms as he, strikingly, refers to this need for expansion by saying that the building was so crowded that the women were forced to walk on the heads of men in order to reach the altar. Love's need to have room to move provides the subtext for the renovation of the abbey church of Saint-Denis. His meditation on the beauty of the gems and the subsequent transport to the realm of understanding is thus seen to be motivated by love. But unlike the love of Augustine, which turns away from the world in pursuit of the divine, Suger's understanding of both amplification and dwelling, aided by the glosses of Hugh of Saint Victor, is securely rooted in the things of this world. The abbey church is grand and beautiful because love needs room to move.

To turn, then, to the deployment of these concepts in a literary context, one finds the same cluster of dwelling, amplification, and love occurring with great frequency in the poems of the troubadours.

3. Dwelling on a Point

These poets, who thrived in the south of France and wrote in the Romance tongue of Occitan, are credited with initiating the burgeoning vernacular literary tradition that started in the twelfth century in Europe. Little is known about these early poets: much of what is asserted about them is in fact drawn from fictional 'lives' that contain little truth. The poems cover many topics – politics, loss, friendship – in many different genres, including dawn songs, debates, eulogies. But the majority of the poems are of a type called *canso*, or song, and focus on love. This love, which can be chaste or carnal, is nonetheless intimately tied up with the process of singing, and the link between language and love is strongly asserted. Moreover, what links all of these songs, apart from the fact that they are written in the same vernacular, is that they all follow an intricate rhyme pattern; the effect of such strict and complicated rhyming is to foreground the use of language in a way that emphasizes its materiality. The symmetry of the rhymes makes objects, spaces, of the poems. Take, for instance, the following *cobla*, or stanza, from 'Lanquan vei fueill'e flor e frug' ('When I see leaf and flower and fruit') of the troubadour Arnaut Daniel (fl. 1180-1210), whom Dante credits with being the 'better maker of the mother [read 'vernacular'] tongue'. Arnaut is known in particular for his elaborate rhyme schemes:

> Ar sai ieu c'Amors m'a condug
> E sieu plus seguran castel.
> Don non dei renda ni trahug –
> Ans m'en ha fait don e capdel
>
> Now I know that love has led me
> Into her castle held most securely
> Where I do not need to pay rent or tribute –
> Rather she has made me lord and master.

Love as a presence needs space to thrive. The pairing of an architectural space, in which one can commune with oneself or explore love with one other, surfaces throughout medieval vernacular literature.

In the thirteenth-century *Romance of the Rose*, for instance, the garden that is finally breached offers such a space; in the twelfth-century lais of Marie de France one finds again and again the creation of a space associated with love. Most strikingly, as one moves higher and higher through Dante's *Divine Comedy* of the fourteenth century, one finds the formal structure of the poem – which turns around the three-line verse or stanza (which means 'room') as Dante himself calls it – being echoed in the creation of spaces that enable the discussion of love. None exists in *Inferno*; in *Purgatorio* the ledges of the mountain suggest the immanence of such spaces; in *Paradiso* enclosing spaces become more prevalent as love infuses celestial space.

While for Augustine love offers an escape from the body and strictures of this world, by the high Middle Ages love is intimately involved with space, and language is shown capable of creating spaces analogous to these where love can flourish. *Commoratio* as a dwelling is indeed the critical notion behind this. Troubadour poems themselves, like the process of reading and Suger's of dwelling, enact the trope of *commoratio*. Take, for example, another song by Arnaut Daniel, 'Lo ferm voler', which is a sestina – the first of its kind. A sestina is a poem of thirty-nine lines (six six-line stanzas and usually one three-line final stanza, or *tornada*). Here the same six words – *ongla, vergua, cambra, oncle, arma, intra* – occur at the end of each six-line stanza in a prescribed – and changing – order, with the echo of all six words coming together in the *tornada*. Throughout the poem the six words take on different meanings depending on their context; at the end they are linked narratively, in the final three-line stanza:

> Arnauts tramet sa chansson d'ongl'e d'oncle,
> A grat de lieis que de sa verg'a l'arma,
> Son Desirat cui pretz en cambra intra,

Arnaut sends his song of nail and uncle, by the grace of her who has the soul of his rod, his desired one, who enters the bedroom with prowess.

3. Dwelling on a Point

The focus on the six words, five of which can occur as nouns, are teased out to create the poem. These key words generate the sense of the poem, even as they establish the poem's structure, and the closed unit the poem offers creates a space where love can thrive. What we see with the troubadours that we did not see in the treatises or with Suger is how the material qualities of the language itself become the means for amplification, and how those rhetorical devices are, in turn, reflected in the thematic of the poems. A comparable reflexive quality between form and theme can be found in the English sestina by Rudyard Kipling, 'Sestina of the Tramp-Royal':

> Speakin' in general, I 'ave tried 'em all –
> The 'appy roads that take you o'er the world.
> Speakin' in general, I 'ave found them good
> For such as cannot use one bed too long,
> But must get 'ence, the same as I'ave done,
> An' go observin' matters till they die.
>
> What do it matter where or 'ow we die,
> So long as we've our 'ealth to watch it all –
> The different ways that different things are done,
> An' men an' women lovin' in this world;
> Takin' our chances as they come along,
> An' when they ain't, pretendin' they are good?
>
> In cash or credit – no, it aren't no good;
> You've to 'ave the 'abit or you'd die,
> Unless you lived your life but one day long,
> Nor didn't prophesy nor fret at all,
> But drew your tucker some'ow from the world,
> An' never bothered what you might ha' done.
>
> But, Gawd, what things are they I 'aven't done?
> I've turned my 'and to most, an' turned it good,
> In various situations round the world –

For 'im that doth not work must surely die;
But that's no reason man should labour all
'Is life on one same shift – life's none so long.

Therefore, from job to job I've moved along.
Pay couldn't 'old me when my time was done,
For something in my 'ead upset it all,
Till I 'ad dropped whatever 'twas for good,
An', out at sea, be'eld the dock-lights die,
An' met my mate – the wind that tramps the world!

It's like a book, I think, this bloomin' world,
Which you can read and care for just so long,
But presently you feel that you will die
Unless you get the page you're readin' done,
An' turn another – likely not so good;
But what you're after is to turn 'em all.

Gawd bless this world! Whatever she 'ath done –
Excep' when awful long – I've found it good.
So write, before I die, ''E liked it all!'[22]

The link between reading and living, nascent in the troubadour songs, is here made explicit, and the material aspects of the language are played out through the aural repetition of the final words.

Another example of how the form of troubadour poetry often emphasizes presence in the world can be found in Raimbaut d'Aurenga's 'Assaz m'es belh'. Raimbaut, whose dates are placed in the mid- to late twelfth century, was, like Arnaut, a master of the use of rhyme and clever wordplay in Occitan.

Assaz m'es belh
Que de novelh
Fassa parer
De mon saber
Tot plan als prims sobresabens

Que van comdan
Qu'ab sen d'enfan
Dic e fatz mos captenemens;
E sec mon cor
E·n mostri for
Tot aisso don ilh m'es cossens.

Qui qu'en favelh,
Lo m'es pro belh
De mon saber:
Qu'en sai mielhs ver
(Sitot no suy mout conoyssens)
Que·l trop parlan
Que van comdan
'Folhs es'. – 'non es'. – 'si es sos sens'.
Qu'ar tost salh for
Ab belh demor
Gen motz leugiers, cortes, valens.

Ab sen novelh
Dic e favelh
Mon saber ver
E·l fas parer
Lay on tanh que sia parvens;
Que son enfan
Li mielhs parlan
Vas me; e sai qui·m n'es guirens,
Ab que·m demor
Gen dins mon cor
Si que·l dir no·m passa las dens.

Don d'amar dic:
Qu'am si ses tric
Lieys qu'amar deg,
Que·l miels adreg

(S'eron sert cum l'am finamens)
M'irion sai
Preguar hueymai
Que·ls essenhes cum aprendens
De ben amar;
E neus preguar
M'en venrion dompnas cinc cens.

Ben ai cor ric
Plus qu'ieu non dic
E tan adreg
Que ducx ni reg
No prez, si no·m prez'eissamens;
A cuy no·m play,
Ieu suy de say;
Et amarai mos bevolens.
No vuelh preguar,
Que miels m'er car
Q'om mi prec, qu'ieu prec manhtas gens.

L'enojos tric,
Sian del ric
Sobeiran reg
Maudig, e deg
Dels janglos parliers maldizens!
Gic m'en hueymai,
Que·l dir no·m plai
Tan m'es lur mentaure cozens!
Que s'il tug car
Meron, amar
No·ls poiria, que·l cor m'en vens.

Pauc sap d'amar
Qui tem preguar
Deu, qu'el maldia los manens.
E·t voill pregar,

Vers, ab diz car
Que lai en Urgel te prezens,

Ab talen car
Si·m fai amar.
E·l bon esper qu'eu n'ai guirens![23]

It is quite lovely to me that again I may cause my learning to appear clearly to the fine know-it-alls who are spreading rumors that I speak and act like an infant; and I follow my heart and show forth all that she allows.

Whoever may debate it, I am quite happy with my knowledge: for I know the truth about it (even though I don't know much) better than the chatty ones who go around saying: 'he's crazy', – 'no, he isn't' – 'but what he says is'. For presently out come, with fine demeanour, humane words, light, courtly, meaningful.

With new understanding I speak and discuss my true knowledge and cause it to appear there where it is appropriate, for the best speakers are but infants compared to me, and I know who is my patron in this matter, provided that that [knowledge] remains safe in my heart so that no word escapes my teeth.

And so I talk about love: since I love without tricks the one I should love, the most adept lovers, if they knew how charitably I loved her, would come here to beg me to take them on as students of true love, and five hundred ladies would also come to beg me for it.

Indeed I have a more moral heart than I say and am so adept that I don't abide either duke or king who doesn't abide me equally; for the one I don't like, I stand apart; and I will love my well-wishers. I do not care to pray, for I would rather be prayed to than do the praying.

May the annoying tricks be cursed by the noble sovereign king, along with the sins of the slanderous, gossiping speakers. I'll change the subject for I don't like to talk about it, so painful is its mention. For even if they were all to take vengeance on me, I couldn't love them, since my heart overcomes me.

He knows little about love who fears to pray God to curse the players.

And I pray you, verse of precious words, show yourself there in Urgel,

With precious desire, so make me loved; and I expect good, for I have the patron for it.

Here we find a beautifully complex rhyme scheme that matches not the diction of the poem so much as its meaning. A poem of six stanzas and three *tornadas*, or final transmitting sets of lines, the rhyme remains consistent through the first three stanzas; then through the second three; and the *tornadas* repeat the final rhymes of those second three stanzas. Within this structure more complicated variations occur: while the opening couplet of each three *coblas* use the same rhyme sound, the actual rhyme word progresses from first to second place (*dic/tric* in the first becomes *ric/dic* in the second and *tric/ric* in the third). The same is true of the couplet in the middle of each stanza (*sai/huemai*; *play/say*; *hueymai/plai*); while the reverse occurs in the last two lines (*amar/ pueguar*; *pueguar/car*; *car/amar*). In each case the forward progress is stopped by the fact that the word introduced in the last pairing occurred first in the initial set. The lines close in on themselves, and the effect of reversing the direction of the flow in the last lines only serves to reinforce this sense of closure.

To a large extent, this poem is nothing but rhyme. The lines are short, the words simple, direct, and limited in number, as not just rhymes but words and whole lines are repeated verbatim. That simplicity is paired, however, with a sophistication of understanding ('Lo m'es pro belh/ De mon saber/ Qu'en sai mielhs ver ... Que·l trop parlan'). The poet's superior knowledge, which comes from 'following his heart', leads him to produce words that are well chosen.

In this textual space the poet proposes to reveal his knowledge to the public who want to be his students but also, unfortunately, to those who claim to know more than he does. He speaks, but the harboured words become curses against those who speak ill of him. He aims to speak wisdom through sweet song, but the sweetness is, at least on the level of plot, lost, or almost. He curses instead of pleasing. But the song does do one thing right: it sings of love, which it posits as the product of good words ('don d'amar dic') and those words are repeatedly, strikingly, palpable, both in the rhyme and in the language used of them – they leap forth, they are made to appear, etc. What the poem says of the words is made evident through the structure the rhyme creates as well as through the conceptual space the poem carves out to make itself *prezens* there at Urgel.

Rhymes and love

Faral's book collects major medieval Latin works on writing poetry. But there exist similar works in the vernacular, keyed to composing in the mother tongue. The fourteenth-century *Leys d'Amors* (*Laws of Love*) is one such work, in which troubadour song is described and the process of vernacular composition is laid out in detail. The *Leys* exist in two major editions, one of which is more detailed than the other.[24]

The *Leys* state clearly that rhyme is a constitutive element of *trobar*, or creating verse: prose works, such as the roman de Saint Graal, it says, differ from troubadour song in their lack of metre, measure, and rhyme. The science of *trobar*, the text adds, was founded so that the compositions would be more pleasing 'per los rims'. The *Leys* are clear that rhyme does not refer just to the final syllable but, instead, to the line as a whole. Rhyme, the *Leys* tell us, determines the shape of both the line and, from that, the stanza and is thus a key structural element of the poem.

But the fifth part of the standard Gatien-Arnoult edition of the *Leys* elaborate on the role of rhyme as it asserts a connection between word choice and love. This section aims to teach anyone who wants to *trobar* in the vernacular how it is done and to teach lovers how they are to love and what constitutes good love: 'for never has a good troubadour who has been a loyal lover been involved in vicious love or dishonest desire'.[25] But then, and this is critical, the notion of *trobar* is qualified as rhyming: this section, it says, will start by showing how one can 'dictar e far rimas acordans'.

The central role granted rhyme is affirmed through the following metaphor:

Et en aquesta maniera de dictar deu hom far coma fan li teysshedor, qui primieramen apparelho et ordissho los fils e pueysh teyssho lo drap. Quar primieramen si hom vol far una canso o un vers . . . hom deu primieramen sercar quatre manieras de rims, si tant es que en cascuna cobla sian viii bordo.[26]

And in this manner of composing we perform like weavers who first prepare and warp the thread and then weave the cloth. For first of all if you want to make a canso or vers ... you must identify four types of rhyme, if you have eight lines per stanza.

Like the warp of a tapestry, the rhyme defines the song. The treatise is explicit that the poet should choose the rhymes first – taking care not to choose sounds that are too hard to rhyme – and then weave in the subject: 'Pauzat havem nostre ordimen dels rims e mostrat per qual maniera los deu hom sercar e trobar, *donx aras es hora que cercam e fassam nostre dictat*' ('We have established the warp of the rhymes and shown how we are to find and compose them; now we will show how to find and create the tapestry that is the poem'; emphasis mine).

The purpose and function of rhyme are thus clarified in the treatise. The rhyme words lay the groundwork for the figure that is the subject. What the poems offer is the spatial organization of speech, and rhyme does not so much organize the flow as it shapes the words, turning them, giving them dimension. 'Et en ayssi hom que dicta deu tantas vetz trasmudar las dictios e una metre per autra e virar so denan detras e pel contrari'[27] ('Therefore, one who composes must often transmute words, switch one for another, and put one behind another and vice versa').

Love makes you a better person

Rhyme creates a space much as *commoratio* does. But the troubadour poems add one further element to the mix, as they bring us back to the Ciceronian notion that rhetoric serves to define the good. These poems cover a range of topics and address a variety of audiences, but what stands out about them is that they are minimalist in their representation and they employ complex rhyme schemes through which they advance the notion that singing about love makes you a better person. What is implicit in the example of Geoffrey and Suger is explicit in troubadour song: for the troubadours, love makes you a better singer. In other words, the rhetorical system of Cicero and Quintilian, though narrowed to focus on style and poetry, nonetheless maintains its roots in ethical activity. Poetry is rhetorical because it is a means for ennoblement.

The most anthologized and most translated troubadour, Bernart de Ventadorn (*c*. 1150-80), is also clearest in his linking of love and honour. Unlike Arnaut and Raimbaut, Bernart's interest lies more in developing themes than in clever and artful wordplay. As a result, his poems are useful for grasping the concepts that engage the troubadour poet.

> Chantars no pot gaire valer,
> Si d'ins dal cor no mou lo chans;
> Ni chans no pot dal cor mover,
> Si no·i es fin'amors coraus.
> Per so es mos chantars cabaus,
> Qu'en joi d'amor ai et enten
> La boch'e·ls olhs e·l cor e·l sen.

Singing cannot be worth much if the song does not come from within the heart; nor can the song come from the heart unless there is there heartfelt, noble love. And so my singing is the tops, for in love's joy I hold and direct my mouth and my eyes and my heart and my comprehension.

The connection Bernart makes here between singing and love he reiterates elsewhere, as do other troubadours, including Raimbaut d'Aurenga. As Bernart writes: 'Non es meravelha s'eu chan/ melhs de nul autre chantador,/ que plus me tra·l cors vas amor/ e melhs sui faihz a so coman' ('It's no wonder that I sing better than any other singer, since my heart draws me more toward love and I am made better by its command'). This adapts the basic tenet of Roman rhetoric, that speaking well depends on acting well, while acting well, or morally, enables you to speak well: a skilled orator is a good man (*vir bonus*). In troubadour poetry, love has replaced the good of Roman rhetoric. Singing well is a function of loving: love and song bear the same reciprocal relationship in troubadour verse that speech and the morally good do in Roman rhetoric. This much we see in both Raimbaut and Bernart and elsewhere.

Conclusion

The *artes poeticae* of the high Middle Ages see a crossover between Ciceronian rhetoric and Augustinian thought:[28] love is uplifting because love is rhetorical. Because of the intervening introduction of love into the discourse on persuasion – because of the centrality of love to Christian doctrine – speaking well becomes involved with speaking love and it is the language of love that becomes capable of order. The twelfth century, then, marks a return to the rhetoric of Cicero, with a twist; the rhetorical system emerges intact, yet the setting has changed. We are no longer looking for the rhetoric that enables community in the forum or the courtroom: instead, rhetoric shows up in discussions of love, and love in the discussions of rhetoric. Current scholarship on troubadour poetry in particular has isolated love not as the object of the poet's affection but as 'the very possibility of language'; and the origin of vernacular song can be seen to derive from the philosophical tradition of Neoplatonic study during the twelfth century. I would argue that this approach proves fruitful for rhetoric as well: as much as Plato is distrustful of rhetoric, Neoplatonic thought, particularly as filtered through Augustine and developed in grammatical studies of the eleventh and twelfth centuries, allowed for the marriage of love and rhetoric, and enabled rhetoric to create a situation in which love could prevail. Love understood as 'the pure potential of language' or, in Augustine's terms, 'the motion of the soul toward God', which is pursued through textual interpretation, becomes the manifestation of rhetoric apparent in the treatises and literary works of the time. But in the works of the twelfth century, love becomes rooted in the spaces of this world: *commoratio*, rhyme and figures in general provide ways to create the space for love. Whereas in classical rhetoric a good man is one who speaks well, in the high Middle Ages a good man is one who loves well.

The works of the troubadours offer examples of using love to enable community – of using love rhetorically. The critical point about *amour courtois* is often overlooked: it suggests that man can be humanized by the language of love, where the emphasis is on the use of language and so marks the re-emergence of a classical rhetorical mode, set in a new key. The affiliation of *amour courtois* and ancient rhetoric, then, is not a fluke. Courtly love marks the adaptation of rhetoric to new ends; it signals the organization of *caritas* as a means toward a secular community capable of ennoblement through language, where the central model is not speaking but reading.

The rhetorical tradition enables love to intersect with the material concerns of the world – hence the emphasis on dwelling and lingering. Augustine emphasizes the power of love to transport the soul away from the world toward God. Suger's interest in lingering in his renovated chapel in order to enable its beauty to transport him speaks to a slight but significant shift in focus. The motion of delight is now through rather than away from the material. The *artes poet-*

icae of the twelfth and thirteenth centuries, and the poetry they inspire, speak as well to the power of love to transform through language, in all its physical and material presence.

4

The Chiastic Page: The Rhetoric of Montaigne's *Essais*

Figures take centre-stage in European rhetoric of the sixteenth century, and rhetorical treatises of this time struggle between growth and stasis, between wanting to portray the inner self, particularly the emotions, and acknowledging the difficulty or impossibility of doing just that. In Michel de Montaigne's hands, the rhetorical project of his *Essais* becomes a dual one: representing himself accurately on the pages of his work, which, in turn, plays out as a struggle between text and margin. Rhetoric – which has become 'the ability to move affections through language' – is in Montaigne's time taken over by literature, as the 'whole force and energy of classical rhetoric' as performing art is assumed by the written text.[1] The interest in moving affections is reflected in a literary interest in portraying them: the will to move affections through language becomes thematized in literature as the representation of the affections and emotions in language. As with the earlier eras, this contradiction shows up in the contrast between how the treatises say what they are proposing to do and how they actually go about doing it, but what is different here is that the page itself becomes the forum for this particular conflict. And, as we have seen in earlier chapters, the contradictions that surface in the treatises are played out in the literature of the time. Nowhere is the tension between growth and stasis played out better on the space of the page than in the writing of Montaigne.

The tension is represented most clearly by the figure of chiasm. The name derives from the Greek letter X, chi, since the figure works by inverting terms. That chiasm surfaces as the key figure, at least in the literature after that time, has been shown by John Hollander, who points out in *Melodious Guile* that the specular figure of chiasmus (a:b::b:a) 'has [by the Renaissance] come to be a scheme of schemes':

> there is … something deeply compelling about this myth of chiasm as mirror. … The mirror is human thinker, transient and mortal like that which he or she reflects and reflects upon.[2]

Hollander isolates the possible *locus classicus* in John Milton (1608-74) where the description of Eve seeing her own image is expressed in chiastic terms (*Paradise Lost* 4.460-2):

> As I bent down to look, just opposite
> A shape within the watery gleam appeared
> Bending to look on me …

Yet the examples abound. Take, for example, this letter from Milton's contemporary, the Puritan author Anne Bradstreet (1612-72), to her son, written in 1664:

> Parents perpetuate their lives in their posterity and their manners; in their imitation children do naturally rather follow the failings than the virtues of their predecessors, but I am persuaded better things of you. You once desired me to leave something for you in writing that you might look upon, when you should see me no more; I could think of nothing more fit for you nor of more ease to myself than these short meditations following. Such as they are I bequeath to you.[3]

The 'I bend-down-look: bend-down-look me' Hollander identifies in the Milton is echoed by the 'You desired me: I desired [think of nothing more fit for] you' of the Bradstreet. Both Milton and Bradstreet link chiasmus with specularity – in the structure of sentences, in the essential meaning – that functions on surface and sublexical levels.

Chiasm, Hollander makes clear, was initially only a figure of speech. By the time of Milton, though, it had penetrated into the deeper levels of consciousness, had become a figure of thought, as it represented critical cultural questions. The inversion embedded in chiasm, however, is apparent both in earlier rhetorical treatises and in the writing of Michel de Montaigne. In each, chiasm surfaces as a form of amplification prompted or at least supported by the appearance of the text on the page.

A sampling of rhetorical treatises

Sixteenth-century British rhetorical treatises are particularly marvellous documents to study. In Thomas Wilson's *Art of Rhetoric* (1553)[4] as later for Henry Peacham, the purpose of troping and rhetoric is to link the bodily experience to the life of the mind. But while Peacham discusses amplification in his section on tropes, Wilson discusses it in his section on memory. Memory, he says, 'is to the mind as life is to the body. ... [It] is the power of the mind that containeth things received, that calleth to mind things past, and reneweth of fresh things forgotten'. To this he adds a telling variant on the ancient methods of memorization. In order to memorize, he states, you must have a place and an image. At first he says that the place is like the wax or the paper, the image like letters or a seal, but then he suggests that the place can be body parts.

Linking the body to the page draws Wilson strikingly close to Peacham: for each, rhetoric exists to draw the body on the page, to create through words the experience of the body to the greatest extent possible in order, finally, to enable the text to affect the emotions. The *Garden of Eloquence* (1577) of Henry Peacham[5] distinguishes under the heading of 'a figure what it is' the major categories of trope and 'schemates'. Within 'schemates' he distinguishes repetition, omission, conjunction, separation. He then identifies two types of figures, of sentences and of words, where the former are 'manly and martiall', the latter 'effeminate and musicall'. Where figures of sentences give life and affection to writing, figures of words add colour and beauty. Under figures of sentences he includes two subcategories, affection and amplification, where affection includes exclamations and amplification, garnishments.

And yet, when Peacham gets into the body of the work, he redivides this taxonomy, placing amplification in a category all its own, on a par with figures of sentences and figures of words. No longer just a footnote or subcategory, amplification stands alone. Peacham defines amplification as 'artificial and cunning instruments apt and ready to amplify and garnish with speech any causes or purpose which man's wit can invent or his capacity conceive: for things by distribution are set forth plentifully, by description evidently, by comparison amply, and by collection strongly'. Amplification, he continues, serves as 'affirmation very great and weighty which by large and plentiful speech moveth the minds of the hearers and causeth them to believe that which is said'. In this, he uses the treatise to exemplify the figure, even as the treatise undoes its assertion of clarity. Amplification, this suggests, has a life of its own which overwhelms any efforts at restraint or clarity.

The fact that amplification erupts through the body of the treatise speaks, of course, to the nature of the figure. It also, however, speaks to a tension commonly found in Renaissance treatises between order and growth. Peacham orders the figures only to have that order disrupted, the categories reworked by one rogue figure. The more the treatises try to order, it would appear, the more that effort is reciprocated by the need for language to express and emote.

In the earlier rhetorical treatise *Tabulae de schematibus et tropis* of Mosellanus (Petrus Schade, 1493-1524),[6] a rhetorician who had commented on the recently rediscovered *Institutes* of Quintilian, we find an emphasis on multiplication. Here, in the discussion of figures, we find a list of common terms: metaphor, catechresis, metonymy, etc. The list is supplied at the start, but when the discussion begins, the list grows in a lopsided fashion: instead of moving from allegory to periphrasis as the prelude tells us it will, it adds in subsets of allegory, such as enigma and irony. So, also, two figures later, hyperbaton is not immediately followed by hyperbole but, instead, by a list of related figures, including anastrophe, dialysis, and hysteron proteron. Finally, the list, which should have ended with homoeosis, ends instead with variants of that figure, including icon, parabole, and paradigma.

So we have lists that grow in the telling, one term breeds another, and the order proposed at the start is complicated by the end. The surface simplicity suggested at the beginning of the treatise is undone by the end, and the reader is left with a sense that the depths have just begun to be plumbed. For even as the list grows organically, so, like an early flow chart, one thing leads to a plethora of others. Peacham and Mosellanus share both the tendency to suggest that what their treatise will offer is simple and clear, and the need to amplify and elaborate that clarity as the text develops. Where they differ is that Peacham reorganizes while Mosellanus elaborates. It is striking that both are examples of amplification, and both seem drawn to a demonstration of amplification in rhetorical terms, Peacham elevating it to the level of category, Mosellanus enacting it within the structure of the treatise. Amplification, it would seem, retains the power it had in twelfth-century texts and treatises, even as the rhetoricians try to suggest otherwise by burying it in the midst of their treatises. Its very inability to be categorized – or, conversely, its ability to undo the categories established, somewhat like a computer virus – suggests its innate power and importance.

Yet the precise nature of this amplification clearly differs from that of the earlier texts. Amplification, as Peacham reminds us, provides 'affirmation very great and weighty' which moves the mind of hearers and causes them to believe what is said. This figure is no longer what it was in the twelfth century. As Shakespeare's personification of amplification in the character of Bottom in *A Midsummer Night's Dream* makes clear, this figure is about wit and invention. Not only does this leader of the 'rude mechanicals' embody amplification in his physical stature (the wit of the line 'Masters, spread yourselves' is heightened through this) but his overblown style, both in his conversation with his men and in the delivery of his lines, reflects the nature of the trope of amplification. It is the very soul of rhetoric – that it shares with its twelfth-century archetype – but the nature of the being has changed drastically.

Amplification and the senses

Peacham's treatise treats tropes and schemes and the ways in which they make words and sentences 'new by art'. He is very clear how this is done. First and foremost, tropes and schemes derive from external senses of the body which are then compared to an internal virtue of the mind. He hierarchizes the senses: first comes sight, then smelling, feeling or touching, and, finally, tasting. The key move here is comparison: the drive in troping, in making new by art, is to compare; the second key factor is that these comparisons are rooted in the senses of the body. Through troping, Peacham suggests, the world is accommodated to the speaker even as it becomes an extension of the speaker's most basic experiences. Language becomes a way to find oneself in the world at large.

Throughout Peacham's *Garden of Eloquence* we find an insistence on amplification understood as increase and expansion of this particular sort. Inherent in this understanding of rhetoric, however, lies a contradiction that surfaces in the efforts of the treatises to define the function of figures. In the *Arte of English Poesie* (1589), George Puttenham likens figures first to embroidery on clothing or gold on a princely garment and finally to the act of not just a painter, but a portraitist:

> As th'excellent painter bestoweth the rich Orient coulours upon his table of pourtraite … wherfore the chief prayse and cunning of our Poet is in the discreet using of his figures, as the skillful painters is in the good conveyance of his coulours and shadowing traits of his pensill, with a delectable varietie, by all measure and iust proportion, and in places most aptly to be bestowed.[7]

The emphasis on sight is here coupled with an interest in capturing life on the page, best displayed through not just painting, but specifically the painting of portraits. If the endeavour of the Renaissance entails coping 'with its own separation from its imputed sources and masters [in which] each work, each essay [becomes] a vulnerable extension out of the remote into a self-creating, self-vindicating present',[8] the amplitude that pervades both rhetorical treatises on figures is shaped by a chiastic tension with the fixity of the portrait the texts are trying to depict. Amplification emerges as the key figure, but it is amplification within certain bounds: growth with a purpose and a focus that is perhaps best approached in terms of chiasm.

Nowhere is this clearer than in the *De Copia* of Erasmus, Dutch humanist and rhetorician. In this work, first published in 1512, the praises of amplification and eloquence are sung concisely. Likening eloquence to clothing, which is apt and fitting (ch. 10), Erasmus provides instruction on how best to present a topic. A treatise on eloquence, *De Copia* is also a treatise that introduces abundance in the context of appropriateness. Although Erasmus likens *copia* to a stream, it is a golden stream, with an emphasis on the preciousness of that abundance. *De Copia* is a discussion of the method of amplification; as such it offers an approach to abundance that derives from a chiastic tension between expansion and restriction.

Montaigne's *Essais* as rhetoric

Erasmus was steeped in ancient rhetoric, but particularly interested in the works of Quintilian. Erasmus plays a central role in the thinking of French essayist Michel de Montaigne. Through the work of Erasmus, Montaigne comes to an appreciation of the vision Quintilian offers in his *Institutes* of a world improved by language. Yet Montaigne's relationship to Quintilian is complex, since he finds that the world he aims to portray fails, finally, to be captured by that very language. Montaigne's interest in Quintilian is evident not only in his citations from the *Institutes* but also, I will argue, in the form and style he gives the *Essais*.

On the face of it, nothing could be more different than the *Essais* and the *Institutes*. Montaigne, a Gascon retired from public life at the age of thirty-eight (though elected, repeatedly, to public office thereafter, and involving himself in the debate that fueled the civil wars between the Catholics and Protestants), writes in the late sixteenth century of himself for himself. Quintilian, a public servant, writes a handbook of education in the first century CE for the young Roman. One is purportedly descriptive, the other didactic. Yet their approaches are in fact comparable since each roots his observation in the rhetorical. Language, and the conviction that language, because of its history, can mould both ethics and culture, lie at the heart of each text. Moreover, both Montaigne and Quintilian are persuaded that the artistic deployment of language through figures is effective because it is rooted in history.[9]

There are points in Montaigne's text where he seems to be responding directly to Quintilian. As we saw in the first chapter, Quintilian's description of figures is telling: 'the analogy is now with sitting, bending forwards, or looking back' (*sicut nos sedemus, incumbimus, respicimus*) (*Institutio Oratoria* 9.1.11). In the third book of the *Essais*, Montaigne writes: 'Je me presente debout et couché, le devant et le derriere, à droite et à gauche, et en tous mes naturels plis' ('I present myself standing and lying down, front and rear, on the right and the left, and in all my natural postures') (3.8, p. 943; Frame, p. 721).[10] Where Quintilian describes figures through a simile, Montaigne uses a similar series of bodily positions to describe himself, literally. Quintilian's work proceeds in this manner throughout: because of the didactic frame of the text everything is set off, almost as if in quotation marks, and everything is presented at a remove by example. Yet as we have seen, Quintilian's choice of the body is freighted with history: by his time the body had become synonymous with oratory, and the suggestion that figures were manipulations of that body draws on precisely that history. Figures are like a turned body because seemingly direct and literal speech is like a body. The whole rhetorical practice is perceived of and couched in corporeal terms; the body of the speaker and the body of the text join just beyond the margins of Quintilian's text.

For Montaigne, however, those bodies join on the page itself:

C'est icy un livre de bonne foy, lecteur. Il t'advertit dès l'entrée,
que je ne m'y suis proposé aucune fin, que domestique et privée.
Je n'y ay eu nulle consideration de ton service, ny de ma gloire.
Mes forces ne sont pas capables d'un tel dessein. Je l'ay voué à
la commodité particuliere de mes parens et amis: à ce que
m'ayant perdu (ce qu'ils ont à faire bien tost) ils y puissent
retrouver aucuns traits de mes conditions et humeurs, et que
par ce moyen ils nourrissent plus entiere et plus vifve la connoissance qu'ils ont eu de moy. Si c'eust esté pour rechercher la
faveur du monde, je me fusse mieux paré et me presenterois en
une marche estudiée. Je veus qu'on m'y voie en ma façon simple,
naturelle et ordinaire, sans contention et artifice: car c'est moy
que je peins. Mes defauts s'y liront au vif, et ma forme naïfve,
autant que la reverence publique me l'a permis. Que si j'eusse
esté entre ces nations qu'on dict vivre encore sous la douce
liberté des premieres loix de nature, je t'asseure que je m'y fusse
tres-volontiers peint tout entier, et tout nud. Ainsi, lecteur, je
suis moy-mesmes la matiere de mon livre: ce n'est pas raison que
tu employes ton loisir en un subject si frivole et si vain. A Dieu
donq, de Montaigne, ce premier de Mars mille cinq cens quatre
vingts ('Au lecteur', p. 3).

This book was written in good faith, reader. It warns you from
the outset that in it I have set myself no goal but a domestic and
private one. I have had no thought of serving either you or my
own glory. My powers are inadequate for such a purpose. I have
dedicated it to the private convenience of my relatives and
friends, so that when they have lost me (as soon they must),
they may recover here some features of my habits and temperament, and by this means keep the knowledge they have had of
me more complete and alive.

    If I had written to seek the world's favor, I should have
bedecked myself better, and should present myself in a studied
posture. I want to be seen here in my simple, natural, ordinary
fashion, without straining and artifice; for it is myself that I

portray. My defects will here be read to the life, and also my natural form, as far as respect for the public has allowed. Had I been placed among those nations which are said to live still in the sweet freedom of nature's first laws, I assure you I should very gladly have portrayed myself here entire and wholly naked.

Thus, reader, I am myself the matter of my book; you would be unreasonable to spend your leisure on so frivolous and vain a subject.

So farewell. Montaigne, this first day of March, fifteen hundred and eighty (Frame, p. 2.).

Montaigne 'paints' himself as he is, in a simple, natural and ordinary style, without pretence or artifice, and simply decked out: 'paré'. The word is telling, for it is a term that appears often in fifteenth-century poetry to refer to rhetorical colour or figures. His is a simple style, a straightforward one, not heavily embellished with tropes and figures. His later summation, that he paints himself front and back, is alluded to here: if he could, and if the laws of nature allowed, he would paint himself in his entirety – nude, as he says, but also from all sides. 'C'est moy que je peins', he says: he is himself not just the subject about which he writes, he is himself the text that he writes. The metaphor implicit in classical rhetoric that links the body to the text is here made explicit as the body and the text are treated as one.

Montaigne's *Essais* can be approached, I argue, as an inverted rhetorical treatise. Whereas Quintilian's *Institutes* hints at an analogy between body and text, Montaigne sets this equation out from the start: for him the text is not like a body, it is a body, his body, and what happens to it is the essence of rhetoric itself. He is a living metaphor; his wandering and turns should be taken in purely – purely – rhetorical terms. His work as a whole is a figure turned inside out, a metaphor literalized. A comparable approach can be found in the rhetorical writings of Peacham. In his discussion of tropes and schemes Peacham makes it clear that the primary purpose of these devices is to enable an author to discuss the life of the mind: the terms can be taken from an infinite number of places, but primarily they are to be derived from the external sense of the body as compared to an internal virtue of the mind. Here he starts with sight, then moves into smelling, feeling or touching, and tasting. Early on in the *Essais* Montaigne writes:

> Quant aux facultez naturelles qui sont en moy, dequoy c'est icy l'essay, je les sens flechir sous la charge. Mes conceptions et mon jugement ne marche qu'à tastons, chancelant, bronchant et chopant; et, quand je suis allé le plus avant que je puis, si ne me suis-je aucunement satisfaict: je voy encore du païs au delà, mais d'une veuë trouble et en nuage, que je ne puis desmeler (1.26, p. 146).

> As for the natural faculties that are in me, of which this book is the essay, I feel them bending under the load. My conceptions and my judgment move only by groping, staggering, stumbling, and blundering; and when I have gone ahead as far as I can, still I am not at all satisfied: I can still see country beyond, but with a dim and clouded vision, so that I cannot clearly distinguish it (Frame, p. 130).

His *Essais*, it would appear, are efforts at troping; his descriptions are attempts to provide, in precisely the terms Peacham recalls, a sense of the life of the mind through its reaction to the world outside. Where Peacham writes a treatise on similitude, Montaigne writes his *Essais*.

Rhetoric of the *Essais*

'Oyez dire metonomie, metaphore, allegorie, et autres tels noms de la grammaire, semble-t-il pas qu'on signifie quelque forme de langage rare et pellegrin? Ce sont titres qui touchent le babil de vostre chambriere' ('When you hear people talk about metonymy, metaphor, allegory, and other such names in grammar, doesn't it seem that they mean some rare and exotic form of language? They are terms that apply to the babble of your chambermaid') (1.51, p. 307; Frame, p. 223). Style and eloquence, Montaigne argues, are innate. In fact, in the context of the *Essais* as a whole, we find a strong emphasis on the text as a new form of rhetorical treatise: 'Je propose', he writes, 'des fantasies informes et irresolues, comme font ceux qui publient des questions doubteuses, à debattre aux escoles; non pour establir la verité, mais pour la chercher' ('I put forward formless and unresolved notions, as do those who publish doubtful questions to debate in the schools, not to establish the truth but to seek it') (1.56, p. 317; Frame, p. 278). The notion of searching for the truth lies behind the critical action of classical rhetoric: to search is the action of invention, the first and primary act of rhetoric: without invention you have no case, no speech. Invention is the first stage in the rhetorical process. Yet it is striking that Montaigne stops at invention – he does not see it as prelude to anything but instead focuses on the process itself. The process is what matters to Montaigne.

The same can be said of his chapter headings. While, on the face of it, the headings appear to be rhetorical commonplaces or *topoi*, they are anything but. From Aristotle on, *topoi* are common places where two sides of an issue can be discussed. Examples of Aristotelian *topoi* include opposites (If the war is cause of the present evils, things should be set right by making peace); or from the more and less (If not even the gods know everything, human beings can hardly do so). But while the chapter headings of the *Essais* suggest similar rubrics – 'How we cry and laugh at the same things' – the contents and argument that follow is anything but set speeches. As Montaigne himself says,

Les noms de mes chapitres n'en embrassent pas tousjours la matiere; souvent ils la denotent seulement par quelque marque, comme ces autres ... noms, ... J'ayme l'alleure poetique, à sauts et à gambades. ... C'est l'indiligent lecteur qui pert mon subject, non pas moy; il s'en trouvera tousjours en un coing quelque mot qui ne laisse pas d'estre bastant, quoy qu'il soit serré. ... Mon stile et mon esprit vont vagabondant de mesmes (3.9, p. 994).

4. The Chiastic Page

The titles of my chapters do not always embrace their matter; often they only denote it by some sign, like those other ... names. ... I love the poetic gait, by leaps and gambols. ... It is the inattentive reader who loses my subject, not I. Some word about it will always be found off in a corner, which will not fail to be sufficient, though it takes little room. ... My style and my mind alike go roaming (Frame, p. 925).

Rather than denoting commonplaces, the chapter headings denote – often ironically – starting points for philosophical and literary séjours. Again the emphasis on movement and change, again on individuality, again a choice of Montaigne over his stated subject.

Starting from a form that is reminiscent of the rhetorical treatises of old, Montaigne moves into new terrain, one that turns the treatise on its head. One can imagine, playfully, that the *Essais* are in fact the marginalia to Quintilian's *Institutes*: that his style and content are all in response to what Quintilian recommended, and that of all the texts that would have taken centre-stage, the *Institutes* is likely one of the key ones. One of the most resonant echoes between the two texts takes us back to one of the key figures mentioned in Chapter 2. There, in discussing places of uncertainty in Quintilian's taxonomy we talked at length about hesitation and correction, and linked them to larger issues in first-century culture. Correction, as we saw, was key to imperial thought and propaganda, and had as a result moved from being a surface figure to a deep structural principle. By contrast, notice what Montaigne says of correction:

Laisse, lecteur, courir encore ce coup d' essay et ce troisiesme allongeail du reste des pieces de ma peinture. J'adjouste, mais je ne corrige pas (3.9, p. 963).

Reader, let this essay of myself run on, and this third extension of the other parts of my painting. I add, but I do not correct (Frame, p. 894).

This is not, of course, entirely true: we know from the Bordeaux edition that Montaigne did make corrections to his own work. Yet the fact that he perceived himself as not correcting but only adding on sets him in stark contrast to Quintilian and highlights all the more strongly the importance of amplification to his work. Whereas paring down, trimming back, being elliptical, were central to Quintilian's rhetoric and world, adding on – to the ancients, to himself – was key for Montaigne.

Chiasm as a form of amplification

In David Quint's recent reading of Montaigne's first essay, he argues that clemency is central to the *Essais* as it offers 'a new ethics to counter the model of heroic virtue that prevailed in his culture and his noble class. Against the hard-liner who never yields ... he offers a pliant goodness that is the product ... of ordinary fellow feeling. Where the old virtue was autarchic and self-reliant, the new moral behavior that Montaigne advocates is accommodating to other human beings.'[11] One can translate this into the terms we have been discussing, and see Montaigne's efforts to move his personal, disjointed, fluid and changing marginal notes into the centre as stemming from a similar drive. The constant interest in change and adaptation that Montaigne evinces in the *Essais* speaks to both an interest in the humanistic accommodation Quint finds there and the overwhelming sense that the power of language lies not in its use by the 'hard-liners', to use Quint's apt term but, instead, by the ever-changing and adaptive use of the 'chambrieres'. Time and again Montaigne identifies his plight in self-imposed retirement with that of the disenfranchised; but it is in his *Essais* that the disenfranchised become powerful as he sets those identifications in the centre of the page and, through the power of rhetoric, makes the small grand, the marginal central.

From the striking eruption of amplification in Peacham, then, we have moved to an adaptation of amplification by chiasm in Montaigne. Montaigne's efforts are not just to make the small grand, but, at the same time, to reduce the power of the hard-liners, to make the grand small. The poles of this negotiation are reversed for the duration of the *Essais*, and, in Montaigne's assertion that the page is himself, for the extent of our identification with him. It is this action that is so radical and important, and highlights the significance of chiasm: unlike amplification, which, no matter how it is construed, is a process of adding on, chiasm works in two directions at once. In moving his project to the centre of the page, he pushes the tradition out to the margins by reducing it to notes and quotes.

In Montaigne's hands, amplification has been enhanced by chiasm; the central, key figure is now one that entails reversal and transformation as well as accretion. There is a dramatic quality to this that suggests a link between Montaigne's use of chiasm and the flowering of drama in contemporary England: the reversals of fortune that mark Shakespearean plays are based as well on the essential nature of chiasm. One wonders if the chiastic form derives from a certain social mobility, or the frustration at its limitations; in either case the figure would seem to tap into the culture on many levels. While amplification speaks to growth in one direction, chiasm speaks to change and fluidity. Chiasm appears in all treatises preceding the Renaissance, yet it plays only a minor role. It's not until it comes to stand for something more – social mobility, cultural curtailment – that it becomes the prevailing and central figure, as it is in Montaigne's work.

Framing the portrait

Given this, it seems useful to approach the *Essais* by means of the passages where Montaigne describes his project, through the places where he discusses what it is he is aiming to do in writing his book. These descriptions run throughout the course of the *Essais* and throughout its many editions. (Montaigne edited his earlier essays as he wrote the later ones. It has become customary to indicate the strata of edits with the letters a, b, and c; these marks indicate relative stages of revision and completion.) At times Montaigne seems convinced that he will be capable of describing, even capturing, himself. At times, he is much less certain, describing his efforts as surrounding a blank space. Starting with the assertion in the address to the reader that it is himself that he paints, Montaigne suggests throughout the first two books that there is in fact something to paint: 'Je ne dresse pas icy une statue à planter au carrefour d'une ville, ou dans une Eglise, ou place publique. ... C'est pour le coin d'une librairie' ('I am not building here a statue to erect at the town crossroads, or in a church or public square. ... This is for a nook in a library') (2.18, p. 664; Frame, p. 611). Earlier he compares his efforts to those of a painter who depicts him as bald and greying, with his own face, 'non un visage parfaict' (1.26, p. 148). Likening his work to a body (1.26), a figure with one hundred members and faces (1.26), a crowding mass (2.10), a statue (2.18), a painting (1.26, 1.28, 2.6, 2.8, 2.18, 3.2, 3.5, 3.9), a mirror (2.18, 3.5), a bundle of separate pieces (2.37), a drunkard (1.26, 3.2, 3.9), a child (2.8, 3.9), Montaigne makes it clear that on some level at least the subject of his work is in fact a fixable subject.[12]

By the same token, Montaigne undermines the fixity of his subject by insisting throughout that the book is a record of a process (as in 2.17, 3.5 or 2.37). Efforts to see a development from object to process are not entirely convincing. More to the point, I think, is the fact that the book for him is always both a thing and a process – an object that is ever-changing. Perhaps the most useful description he gives of the book, in that it contains elements of thing and process while also linking it to his central metaphor of painting, is the following passage:

> Considérant la conduite de la besongne d'un peintre que j'ay, il m'a pris envie de l'ensuivre. Il choisit le plus bel endroit et milieu de chaque paroy, pour y loger un tableau élabouré de toute sa suffisance; et, le vuide tout au tour, il le remplit de crotesques, qui sont peintures fantasques, n'ayant grace qu'en la varieté et estrangeté. Que sont-ce icy aussi, à la verité, que

crotesques et corps monstrueux, rappiecez de divers membres, sans certaine figure, n'ayants ordre, suite ny proportion que fortuité? ... Je vay bien jusques à ce second point avec mon peintre, mais je demeure court en l'autre et meilleure partie; car ma suffisance ne va pas si avant que d'oser entreprendre un tableau riche, poly et formé selon l'art (1.28, pp. 183).

As I was considering the way a painter I employ [goes] about his work, I had a mind to imitate him. He chooses the best spot, the middle of each wall, to put a picture labored over with all his skill, and the empty space all around it he fills with groteseques, which are fantastic paintings whose only charm lies in their variety and strangeness. And what are these things of mine, in truth, but grotesques and monstrous bodies, pieced together of divers members, without definite shape, having no order, sequence or proportion other than accidental?...I do indeed go along with my painter in this second point, but I fall short in the first and better part; for my ability does not go far enough for me to dare to undertake a rich, polished picture, formed according to art (Frame, p. 164).

The image Montaigne offers is of one painting framed and surrounded by another, the central one being ordered and 'riche, poly et formé selon l'art', the outer one filled with grotesques – fantastic paintings organized without reason or composition. It is this latter type that he likens his own work to, not daring to undertake the tableau in the centre, which he still refers to as the better part ('l'autre et meilleure partie'). Emphasis on the particular that is evident in the earlier comparison with the portrait painter is here complemented by an emphasis on the unruly and unpredictable, a theme Montaigne will return to time and again. His work, unlike that of others, follows no definite and predictable path. Like the grotesques that frame the painting, the *Essais* are valuable only for their 'varieté et estrangeté'.

It is striking that in this passage Montaigne refers to the empty space on the canvas, not, as one might expect, in reference to the central part enclosed by the grotesques, but rather in reference to the space outside the canvas ('et le vuide tout au tour, il le remplit de crotesques'). That this outer area is the space Montaigne himself sees as central is thus made clear. The type of reorientation that Montaigne demonstrates here fits well with the notion that he is turning the exercise of writing inside out – that what is central for others is peripheral to his purpose. Montaigne works in the margins, creating grotesques rather than tableaux: his style, as he says, is 'comique et privé ... inepte aux negotiations publiques ... trop serré, desordonné, couppé, particulier' ('humorous and familiar ... inept for public business ... too compact, disorderly, abrupt, individual') (1.40, p. 252; Frame, p. 252). For the countless 'membres et visages' that every topic has, he considers only a portion: 'Car je ne voy le tout de rien. ... J'y donne une poincte, non pas le plus largement, mais le plus profondement que je sçay' ('I do not see the whole of anything .. I give it a stab, not as wide but as deep as I know how') (1.50, p. 302; Frame, p. 266).

Montaigne's work is off-centre, framing, because the frame is made up of diverse and ill-assorted parts. Where the central canvas is static, the frame is dynamic. The shift in his description from painting a portrait to framing a painting – and from a static topic to a dynamic one – is one that he plays with throughout the *Essais*, and one that offers him a way of presenting his work in the context particularly of earlier rhetorical treatises.

If we think about the *Essais* this way, it produces an interesting result. What Montaigne does is to insist on the marginality – on the difference – of his style over that of the main text. He is not supplanting the main text with his writing. The ancient text remains central, composed, static. His text, like the grotesques in the frame, is something new, something different, something personal. That this is different from the medieval process is heightened by the fact that the central text here is printed, as are the notes; Montaigne's response – handwritten, illegible, personal – stands out as all those things he says of the painter's framing: without definite shape, having no order, sequence or proportion other than accidental. Variety, individuality, organic spontaneous growth all stand as hallmarks of both the marginal notations and the *Essais* as a whole. (One wonders whether Montaigne had in mind the grotesques from the *stanze* of Raphael that he would have seen on his trip to Rome, paintings inspired by the newly rediscovered Golden House of Nero, called grotesques because of their being found in a grotto underground. Raphael's use of the grotesque to fill a wall is similar to Montaigne's use of his commentary: in each case what was originally secondary becomes primary and insists on an aesthetic of its own.)

Our understanding of the image Montaigne probably had in mind has been clarified by the recent 1998 publication of his text of Lucretius.[13] Here we see clearly the image he provides transferred to the written page. In the centre of the page we have the text of Lucretius, interspersed with Lambinus' notes and sigla (these notes are sometimes at the bottom of the page, sometimes in the middle, sometimes at the top). In the margins we see what has been determined to be Montaigne's response to Lucretius – his notes in his handwriting. The notes are copious – often filling the margins, yet not always. He wrote at length about topics that interested him and provided page numbers as cross-references where topics particularly interested him. He read this text when he was thirty-one, in 1564. The *Essais*, started in 1580, seem to be, as he hints they are, an extension of his reading. Moving from the actual to the metaphoric margin Montaigne nonetheless retains the pattern that emerges from reading the Lucretius text: short, underdeveloped notes on reading and experience.

Such a juxtaposition of texts was set in relief more recently by the experiment Jacques Derrida performed in *Glas*. In this essay, Derrida sets two pre-existing texts – one by Hegel, the other by Genet – side by side in an effort to problematize the differences and tensions between the two.[14] As Terence Hawkes writes:

Texts, Derrida's strategy implies, speak with no single, privileged voice, but with one that owes due homage to the work of other texts always covertly juxtaposed with, inserted into, or grafted upon them. In *Glas* one kind of rationality – Hegel's – literally confronts – almost glares at – its opposite, that of Genet: yet, curiously, the one also seems to be shaped by and finally almost dependent upon the other. What first appears as a radical disjunction between the two columns turns gradually into a kind of fruitful connection, something which plunges the very notion of text into a revealing crisis, exposing and bringing into question the process of 'smoothing over the joins' in which our production of meaning has such a massive investment.[15]

In Montaigne the differences are even more strongly felt. Orthography, tone, rhetoric all differ between marginal and central text, in addition to the differences Derrida notes between his two texts. Moreover, while Derrida focuses only on the two columns this exercise offers up on a single page, Montaigne worked across a two-page spread, since he was writing into a pre-existing book. Montaigne's own collection of manuscripts and books suggests that he would have been aware of the physical differences between them; his reiteration of the painting metaphor for his project makes it clear that he was conscious of the page as a canvas, and the margin as the framing white space around the central image. Given this, it seems plausible to suggest that he would have been aware of the graphic layout of the two-page spread, and the fact that his annotations alternated with that of the main text. His marks, in Lucretius at least, are overwhelmingly in the outer, not the gutter margin;[16] the canvas the page offered was one that was inherently chiastic. As he insists on the difference between his text and the central one, as he asserts the pre-eminence or at least comparable *gravitas* of his own work, Montaigne urges the reader to see his texts as comparable to the originating text. In so doing he opens up the possibility of a rhetoric that gains its energy from a dialogue between centre and edge and that is, most importantly, laid out on the page in chiastic fashion.

Let us take stock of what Montaigne has offered us so far: his work, he says, is the scribbles in the margin of another text that he likens to the space around a composed painting. As we know from looking at his Lucretius, this metaphor is realized in his own notation to ancient texts, where 'la vuide tout autour' is filled with his own thoughts and appreciations of the text. The fact that the area around the text, read left to right, creates a dialogue between ancient and modern, between printed and written, often between Latin and French, adds to Montaigne's own statements that what he does is accretion not correction, and that this accretion takes a particular form that is more chiastic than random. The chiastic layout of the page is echoed in his work, where the key phrase 'c'est moy que je peins' embeds the chiasm in the central project. His notes on the flyleaves of the Lucretius support this idea. While he leaves the text of Lucretius markedly untouched, he quibbles with the grammar and rhetoric in detail on the flyleaves. Moreover, while the notes are predominantly in French, the grammatical comments are in Latin. He is his work, but more important, the 'moy' that he paints is a 'moy' of the accreted margins. These margins are separable from the central work, and it is their unfinished quality that distinguishes them from the centre of the page and canvas. The importance granted amplification in contemporary rhetorical treatises is carried over to Montaigne's work even as it is clarified in its use: even as amplification in the treatises erupts from the body of the work, so Montaigne both describes and displays his work as the amplification, the filling out of a void surrounding the stated topic. His distance from the ancients can be charted in his interest in using language that recreates its subject not just in different poses but from different angles, as well as in his rejection of correction. Amplification is key, but it is in its chiastic relationship to another that accretion occurs for Montaigne.

In the Introduction to this book I wrote of the way in which errors of classification often lead to insight into a text's priorities and purposes. In the case of Montaigne it is hard to figure out where the errors are, since, as he states repeatedly, there is no norm to compare this text to. And yet, with the image of the page in our minds and the repeated reference to mirroring and chiasm it seems possible to suggest the following: what can be categorized, listed, fixed in some form is what is omitted from this text. What is included is all that does not fit into categories and types. At first Montaigne suggests this project is useless, and for himself and close acquaintances alone:

> What I write here is not my teaching, but my study; it is not a lesson for others, but for me (Frame, p. 331).

> This is for a nook in a library, and to amuse a neighbour, a relative, a friend, who may take pleasure in associating and conversing with me again in this image (Frame, p. 503).

> I write my book for few men and for few years. If it had been durable matter, it would have had to be committed to a more stable language (Frame, p. 913).

Yet it is the very lack of fixity, of a 'langage plus ferme' that Montaigne soon identifies as his watermark and, as such, as his style:

> Je dois au publiq universellement mon pourtrait. La sagesse de ma leçon est en verité, en liberté, en essence, toute; desdeignant, au rolle de ses vrays devoirs, ces petites regles feintes, usuelles, provinciales; naturelle toute, constante, universelle, de laquelle sont filles, mais bastardes, la civilité, la ceremonie (3.5, pp. 887-8).

> I owe a complete portrait of myself to the public. The wisdom of my lesson is wholly in truth, in freedom, in reality; disdaining, in the list of its real duties, those petty, feigned, customary, provincial rules; altogether natural, constant, and universal; of which propriety and ceremony are daughters, but bastard daughters (Frame, p. 822).

> En fin, toute cette fricassée que je barbouille icy n'est qu'un registre des essais de ma vie, qui est, pour l'interne santé, exemplaire assez à prendre l'instruction à contre-poil (3.13, p. 1079).

To conclude, all this fricassee that I am scribbling here is nothing but a record of the essays of my life, which, for spiritual health, is exemplary enough if you take its instruction in reverse (Frame, p. 1007).

What Montaigne has created here is an anti-treatise, a book that, despite itself, has much to offer the world at large. Precisely because he writes only of himself, precisely because he records the fluctuation of his spirit rather than the facts of his existence, his text, more than others, offers as its central lesson guidance on what it means to be human. From time to time Montaigne makes it clear that here is the true rhetoric, as in:

Quand on m'a dit ou que moy-mesme me suis dict: 'Tu es trop espais en figures. Voilà un mot du creu de Gascoingne. Voilà une frase dangereuse ...Voilà un discours ignorant. Voilà un discours paradoxe. En voilà un trop fol. Tu te joues souvent; on estimera que tu dies à droit, ce que tu dis à feinte.' – Oui, fais-je; mais je corrige les fautes d'inadvertence, non celles de coustume. Est-ce pas ainsi que je parle par tout? me represente-je pas vivement? suffit! J'ay faict ce que j'ay voulu: tout le monde me reconnoit en mon livre, et mon livre en moy (3.5, p. 875).

What I have been told, or have told myself: 'You are too thick in figures of speech. Here is a word of Gascon vintage. Here is a dangerous phrase. ... This is ignorant reasoning. This is paradoxical reasoning. This one is too mad. You are often playful: people will think you are speaking in earnest when you are making believe.' 'Yes,' I say, 'but I correct the faults of inadvertence, not those of habit. Isn't this the way I speak everywhere? Don't I represent myself to the life? Enough, then. I have done what I wanted. Everyone recognizes me in my book, and my book in me' (Frame, p. 809).

It is the paradox of chiasm that defines Montaigne and his project. The more he tries to write in the margins of the world, the more he finds himself at its core. His decision to transfer his marginalia to the centre page makes this clear. What had been pushed to the edges is what Montaigne considers essential, and what had been presented as fixed and central he calls mere ceremony. His *Essais* aim to redress the balance.

Conclusion

In Peacham's discussion of amplification he argues that this figure is 'affirmation very great and weighty which by large plentiful speech moveth the minds of the hearers and causeth them to believe that which is said'. In this he echoes Quintilian, who recalls that the orator, above all, must know how to make small things great and great, small. It is this art of 'raising acts and personal traits above their real dimensions' that is central to judicial and epideictic rhetorics, E.R. Curtius argues in his monumental *European Literature and the Latin Middle Ages*.[17] Phrased in this way, amplification would seem to lie at the heart of the trickster's rhetoric, the very rhetoric Plato found so objectionable – rhetoric as a game of illusions where the important things are downplayed and the less important highlighted; where truth is a negotiable commodity, subject to the whims and needs of the speaker. Yet I would argue that Quintilian and Peacham mean something quite different by their understanding of amplification: rhetoric has the ability to empower speech and move the minds of the audience, and amplification is the prime example of this, since it can present things differently from the way they are usually understood. Taken as such, amplification in Montaigne's hands becomes both the key figure to persuasion and, even more important, a figure that is innately linked to chiasm, since the central move is one of reversing poles. If, in other words, rhetoric can serve to present things as the speaker wishes them to be understood, not as the status quo is used to seeing them, it has the power to change and that power is generated by a chiasmic drive to reverse expectations. Montaigne's moving of the margin to the centre is both an act of amplification, in Peacham's sense of the term, and an act of chiasm. It is also, I would argue, a political statement about his times and a vote in favour of the power of rhetoric – understood not as the 'old' rhetoric presented it, as divorced from the world but, instead, in its 'new' guise, with the power to effect change.

While the examples from Montaigne derive, as Quint has shown, from larger religious, philosophical, and cultural issues, they involve questions of identity as well. Montaigne's positing of the self as ever-changing and identified with the image on the page is one that is clearly picked up by both Milton and Bradstreet in the centuries that follow, and the critical epistemological question has become one of self as defined against the world, both present and future. Bradstreet's use of chiasm not in relation to texts of the past but, rather, in relation to the future is telling: from the medieval interest in amplification as dwelling in and on the present we move to the more interlaced image of chiasm that suggests an interdependence between the present and other times and spaces, be they past or future.

Montaigne's illness pervades the book, as does his sense of his own mortality, yet the purpose of writing, and the power of the chiastic turn, is that it enables him to transcend those limits. This is indeed a 'livre de bonne foy', understood less as a leap of faith than as a tour de force. The goodness Montaigne speaks of is precisely the goodness enabled by rhetoric: language can and does transform in its persuasion and, depending on the speaker, that transformation can and should be an act of ennoblement. The chiasm that pervades the *Essais* is a figure that turns the present toward a future where the fluidity and metamorphic powers of language are allowed to transform the world. Milton's Eve speaks to a similar will, and while Anne Bradstreet's focus is more limited and personal, the idea is similar: the self defined through language can and should engage the world.

Rhetoric, I argued in the Introduction, is always concerned with issues of language and action, which in turn raise larger epistemological questions. What we have seen in the course of these chapters is that the figures of rhetoric enable us to identify how those questions are being addressed. Where man stands in twelfth-century France – backing into a sense of physical presence in the world, a sense of self

defined by limited spatial and temporal coordinates – is best represented by the figure of *commoratio*. Where man stands in Montaigne's
time has more to do with a split in that world, one that argues against
identification with the limitations the world seems to impose.
Montaigne escapes the world in his retirement, and redefines the
matter appropriate for the page by moving his marginal notes to the
centre space. Constant motion and accretion speak to an interest in
life and growth that transcends or at least celebrates powers of the
self beyond the limits of the body. For all his interest in the works of
the past, Montaigne's gaze, like that of Anne Bradstreet, is fixed
securely on the future: 'à ce que m'ayant perdu (ce qu'ils ont à faire
bien tost) ils y puissent retrouver aucuns traits de mes conditions et
humeurs, et que par ce moyen ils nourrissent plus entiere et plus vifve
la connoissance qu'ils ont eu de moy' ('so that when they have lost me
[as soon they must], they may recover here some features of my habits
and temperament, and by this means keep the knowledge they have
had of me more complete and alive') ('Au lecteur', p. 9; Frame, p. 2).

Conclusion

Histories of rhetoric often discuss its place in schools, or its link with other discourses of the times. Discussion of figures is often limited to textual analysis. The purpose of this work is to suggest that these approaches fail to address much of what is crucial about rhetoric. Figures permeate our lives, as they have always done, and the play of figures depends on an ironic view of the world which, in turn, depends on an identification between language and power. But as Baudrillard has pointed out, that power does not derive, ultimately, from the ability to bypass language, which would be necessary – and is possible – in a virtual world. Instead, vital power that taps into the difference between man and machine comes from a recognition that figurative language plays a central function. This power must acknowledge what Baudrillard calls the 'poetic resolution of the world' in which truth is not as much the goal as is humanity.

In a review of Ian McEwan's *Saturday* and Vendela Vida's *And Now You Can Go*, both of which use poetry to prevent an impending act of violence, David Orr writes:

> The scenes they create may be improbable, and they may be a little too insistent on poetry's ability to 'do something', but they get one essential thing right – they show poetry being heard as poetry, on its own merits, with all the attendant confusion and delay. ... The scenes are intimate, the outcomes uncertain, and the characters stumble through them as they would an especially complex Shakespearean sonnet. That's as it should be. If there's one thing that ties good books of poetry together ... it's that they let us enter a private space in which time slows down and possibilities expand. In that space, we're allowed to be

tentative, instead of being asked to sign on the line, answer the phone or pick up a weapon. ...

[W]hen Auden tells us that 'poetry makes nothing happen', he's making a tremendous boast in the form of a dismissal. ... If poetry can't change the world (or save our lives), it does mark a pause in which there's no use for usefulness, and anything can take shape.[1]

To a large extent, this pause is what figures enable. In every case we have examined here, the power of figures has centred on their ability to stop action, whether through repetition, delay, dwelling, or chiasm. Like the poetry Orr discusses above, figures mark a pause in which there is no use for usefulness, in which the good can be dwelt upon, a space in which community can form.

Two contemporary films examine this pause in some detail: *Click* and *Over the Hedge*. In each of these 'the pause' is examined at a nano level. In the first, Adam Sandler is given a remote control that grants him control not just over his appliances but over his life – he can replay a scene or he can enter that pause and change events – change, for instance, the path of a ball. But *Click* explores this potential through its obverse. While the remote is shown to be capable of stopping action, of slowing down the pace of our lives, the movie dwells instead on its ability to fast forward. The protagonist is shown racing through scene after scene of the routine actions that constitute our lives. Before he knows it, he is at death's door; he has been on autopilot through his whole life, missing everything except the highest points. At the very end of the movie he wakes up: it was all a dream; yet the message is clear. If we choose to, we can speed through our lives at such a pace that little of it registers; in this the movie makes an eloquent plea for the importance of slowing down and savouring the moments, even if they're difficult, sad, or boring.

This exploration of the space between takes, retakes, and action is the focus of the funniest scene in the animated film *Over the Hedge*, when the manic squirrel, Hammy, is given caffeine in order to speed him up to such an extent that he can get to the suburbs and back without being trapped. The animation freezes – ludicrously – as he runs faster than both sound and light, thus foreclosing the need for replay or repetition. In his ability to outstrip time he stops it, and in that frozen moment, things change and delight.

The key here is the emphasis on delight. The humanistic impulse depends on play, truth's complement. If rhetoric deals in half-truths, it also deals in possibility. Returning to the origins of rhetoric can remind us of this fact; reading the speeches of Cicero or the treatise of Quintilian can point out to us just how playful one can be. Rhetoric, despite its propensity to cataloguing and rules, is a prescriptive and generative discipline: Cicero and Quintilian, following Aristotle, lay out the possibilities for language and for humans, and those possibilities all involve 'what-ifs'. The fact that subject is not identified with object, that repetition can lead to growth, are not repudiations of our western inheritance, but rather validations of it. In every case the rhetoric of the time centres on figures that derive from the crisis of the time transmuted into transcendent force. And rhetoric is the means by which this is accomplished.

Nobel Laureate Wole Soyinka's 2004 Reith lectures on the 'Climate of Fear' speak to this power of rhetoric and metaphor:

> For an intense period … our airwaves were bombarded with an entrapment piece of monologue of just four words: weapons of mass destruction. It was a sustained demonstration, both as metaphor and prophecy, of how empty such rhetoric can prove, yet how effectively it can blind a people, lead them into a cul-de-sac, securing nearly an entire nation within a common purpose that proves wrongly premised. …
>
> There are moments, it must be admitted, when the imperatives of dialogue appear to be foreclosed. Nevertheless, we dare not stop contrasting the dangers of the monologue with the creative potentials of its alternative, the latter holding out a chance of contracting, if not completely dissipating, our climate of fear … it [is] time to eschew the sterile monologues of the past and cultivate a new spirit of dialogue.[2]

Dialogue, he says, enables community. The proof of this lies in Plato's own use of rhetoric – in his myths and dialogues – and his association between rhetoric and seduction. The *Phaedrus*, as many have pointed out, speaks precisely of this crux. Even as Socrates is slamming the shammery of rhetoric, he is seducing the orator. Rhetoric is working despite itself. In the *Symposium* Agathon's discussion of love, full of rich and potential metaphors, is there to outline the space of truth. More to the point, the definitions truth articulates are set in terms that entail illusion, as Plato shows so well. Anyone who uses language to persuade has a choice: to diminish the difference between subject and object or to insist on retaining that space. In the first lies a language of death – of endings. In the second lies a language based on life, on delay and on beginnings.

In the 2006 movie, *Stranger than Fiction*, the protagonist, Harold Crick (Will Ferrell) starts hearing a narrator's voice in his head as he brushes his teeth, counts the pavement squares, and goes about his lack-lustre life as an IRS auditor. While trying to figure out whose narrative he stars in, he falls in love with a woman he is auditing, Ana Pascal (Maggie Gyllenhaal), a Harvard Law drop-out who bakes cookies as her way to save the world. The two have a chance encounter on a city bus as the narrator (Emma Thompson) intones: 'Into this space Ana Pascal would appear', and she agrees to be nice to Crick, who confessed to having 'o-o-ogled' her, only because he stammered. With this, Crick's life changes: the counting of brush strokes, the adding of figures disappears from the screen and he becomes increasingly a figure of spontaneity and inspiration. At the same time, though, the narrator continues to write him into a tragedy, claiming that she is 'not in the business of saving lives, in fact, just the opposite'.

The movie turns around the concepts of comedy and tragedy, the difference, as we are told by Jules Hilbert, the literature professor played by Dustin Hoffman, being that comedy celebrates the continuation of life, tragedy, the inevitability of death. But as Crick, at Professor Hilbert's instigation, realizes that since he will inevitably die he might as well make his life 'the one he's always wanted', he moves into a space of play and possibility. From the stammering encounter on the bus to a full-fledged love affair with Pascal, Crick starts exploring the spaces between the grids that have governed his life thus far. He buys a guitar and, in a key scene, brings Pascal 'flours': a tray of different types of baking flour for her cookies.

With this, Crick begins a new life. He not only falls in love, and learns to play the guitar, he finds a way to search out and meet the writer and narrator of his plot. Using information on an audit form, he finds the phone number for the narrator, Kay Eiffel, and calls her. As Eiffel types the words 'The phone rings' and 'The phone rings again', it rings twice; and even though she waits beyond the interval for the third ring, as she types 'The phone rings a third time', the ringing phone stops her short. Words and action interact as Eiffel not only talks to but meets her protagonist, and having met him promises to try to avoid killing him. The first draft of her book entails his death, but as she reflects on the fact that she has killed eight people in her earlier novels, and as she types the words 'Harold Crick was de-', she decides to change the ending. Rewriting it, she has Crick survive the accident that would have killed him. As he and Pascal reunite in the hospital she intones:

> As Harold took a bite of Bavarian sugar cookie, he finally felt as if everything was going to be OK. Sometimes, when we lose ourselves in fear and despair in routine and constancy, in hopelessness and tragedy, we can thank God for Bavarian sugar cookies. And, fortunately, when there aren't any cookies, we can still find reassurance in a familiar hand on our skin, or a kind and loving gesture, or a subtle encouragement, or a loving embrace or an offer of comfort: not to mention hospital gurneys, and noseplugs, and uneaten Danish, and soft-spoken secrets, and Fender Stratocasters and maybe the occasional piece of fiction. And we must remember that all these things: the nuances, the anomalies, the subtleties, which we assume only accessorize our days are, in fact, here for a much larger and nobler cause. They are here to save our lives.

These everyday occurrences, which, as the narrator says earlier, are the kind of things that 'would have seemed commonplace', are in fact not so much marks of comedy as of rhetoric. It's the rhetorical flourish of flowers becoming flours, of the rewritten ending that affords a new beginning, of the stammer that provides the space for love that serves this noble cause of saving lives. Humanistic rhetoric derives from the intersection of words and action and retains at its core the goal of ennabling community in the face of the inevitability of death. What fiction and noseplugs share, as Eiffel's final speech makes clear, is the ability to turn the everyday into a 'commonplace', into a figure that captures the essence of who we are. Figures are drawn from the world around us even as they make that world back off, just a little, and provide the space where the good can be brought about through words, and lives, as Eiffel says, can be saved. Like the Jedi mind trick, figures can cause us to 'go home and rethink our lives', but the gesture that accompanies those words is not magical but rhetorical. Rhetoric maps the intersection of language and ethical action and, as such, teaches how to find that turn that will enable us to begin again.

Notes

Introduction

1. Brian Vickers, *In Defence of Rhetoric* (Oxford University Press, 1988).

2. *Adirondack Trails: High Peaks Region*, ed. Tony Goodwin (Adirondack Mountain Club, 2004), p. 88.

3. Mary Douglas and David Hull, *How Classification Works* (Edinburgh University Press, 1992), p. 7.

4. Ibid., p. 6.

5. Eric Cheyfitz, *Poetics of Imperialism* (University of Pennsylvania Press, 1997), p. 38.

1. Weapons of Mass Creation: Repetition versus Replication

1. Ralph Lombreglia, 'Massive Acts of Duplication', *Literary Imagination* 2.3 (2000), p. 312.

2. George Kennedy, *New History of Classical Rhetoric* (Princeton University Press, 1994), p. 6; emphasis mine.

3. Jean Baudrillard, *The Vital Illusion*, Wellek Library Lectures (Columbia University Press, 2000), p. 14.

4. Ibid., p. 71.

5. Ibid., pp. 81, 80.

6. Eric Cheyfitz, op. cit. (above, Introduction, n. 5), p. 38.

7. Plato, *Phaedrus*, trans. H.N. Fowler, Loeb Classical Library 36 (Harvard University Press, 1914 repr. 1982), p. 535.

8. Shirley Sharon-Zisser, 'A Distinction No Longer of Use: Evolutionary Discourse and the Disappearance of the Trope/Figure Binarism', *Rhetorica* 11 (1993), pp. 321-42.

9. Allegra Goodman, 'Pembroke Previsited', *American Scholar* (2004), pp. 142-5.

10. Umberto Eco, *The Mysterious Flame of Queen Loana*, trans. Geoffrey Brock (Harcourt, 2005), pp. 24-5.

11. Ibid., p. 253.

12. Ibid., p. 448.

13. Ibid., p. 449.

14. Ibid., p. 448.

15. *9/11 Commission Report* (Norton, 2004) pp. 288-9.

16. 'Postmodern Warfare: The Ignorance of Our Warrior Intellectuals', *Harper's*, July 2002, pp. 33, 35.

2. Looking Back: Figures of Speech and Thought
in the Roman World

1. Ann Vasaly, *Representations: Images of the World in Cicero's Orations* (University of California Press, 1993), p. 185.

2. Laurent Pernot, *Rhetoric in Antiquity*, trans. W.E. Higgins (Cambridge University Press, 2005), p. 84.

3. Cicero, *The Republic*, trans. C.W. Keyes, Loeb Classical Library 213 (Harvard University Press, 1928 repr. 1977), p. 17.

4. Thomas Habinek, *Ancient Rhetoric and Oratory* (Blackwell, 2005), p. 15.

5. Cicero, *De Oratore*, trans. E.W. Sutton and H. Rackam, Loeb Classical Library 348 (Harvard University Press, 1942 repr. 1979), p. 99.

6. Cicero, *De Inventione*, trans. H.M. Hubbell, Loeb Classical Library 386 (Harvard University Press, 1949 repr. 1976), pp. 5, 7.

7. Vitruvius, *Ten Books on Architecture*, trans Ingrid D. Rowland (Cambridge University Press, 1999), p. 34.

8. Peter Dixon, *Rhetoric* (Methuen, 1974), p. 33.

9. Thomas O. Sloane, *Encyclopedia of Ancient Rhetoric* (Oxford University Press, 2001), p. 309.

10. *Brill's New Pauly: Encyclopaedia of the Ancient World*, ed. H. Cancik and H. Schneider (Brill, 2004), vol. 5, col. 421.

11. Ibid., vol. 5, col. 422.

12. Ibid., vol. 5, col. 423.

13. Ibid., vol. 5, col. 422.

14. Ibid., vol. 5, cols 423-4.

15. Ibid., vol. 5, col. 423.

16. Pernot, op. cit. (above, n. **2**), pp. 159-60.

17. Quintilian, *The Orator's Education*, ed. and trans. Donald A. Russell, Loeb Classical Library 124-7 (Harvard University Press, 2001), vol. 126, p. 353.

18. M.K. Thornton and R.L. Thornton, 'The Financial Crisis of A.D. 33: A Keynesian Depression?', *Journal of Economic History* 50 (1990), pp. 658, 661.

19. *Iliad* 20.200-18; 244-58; trans. W.H.D. Rouse (New American Library, 1964), pp. 240-241. I have adapted the translation slightly.

20. Martha Malamud, 'Gnawing at the End of the Rope', *Ramus* 27 (1998), pp. 95-126.

21. Jamie Masters, *Poetry and Civil War in Lucan's* Bellum Civile (Cambridge University Press, 1992).

22. David Quint, *Epic and Empire* (Princeton University Press, 1993).

23. Michael C.J. Putnam, *Poetry of the* Aeneid (Harvard University Press, 1965), ch. 4; Theodore Ziolkowski, *Hesitant Heroes: Private Inhibition, Cultural Crisis* (Cornell University Press, 2004).

24. Without delay, dying he drew [the sword] from the seething wound. As he lay flat on the ground, the blood shot in the air, just as when a waterpipe whose lead is weak bursts and shoots forth plumes of water from the slender, hissing gap, cutting the air with its spurts. With the shooting blood the fruit of the tree turns crimson, and the roots, soaked with blood, tinged the hanging mulberries a deep red.

25. T.P. Wiseman, *Remus: A Roman Myth* (Cambridge University Press, 1995), pp. 110-11.

26. Paul Allen Miller, *Subjecting Verses* (Princeton University Press, 2004).

27. Stephen Hinds, *Allusion and Intertext* (Cambridge University Press, 1998), ch. 4.

3. Dwelling on a Point: Rhetoric and Love in the Middle Ages

1. Richard McKeon, 'Rhetoric in the Middle Ages', *Speculum* 17 (1942), pp. 1-32.

2. Vickers, op. cit. (above, Introduction, n. 1), ch. 4, esp. pp. 225-31.

3. Vickers, ibid., p. 231, discussing McKeon, op. cit.

4. Joseph M. Miller, Michael H. Prosser, and Thomas W. Benson, *Readings in Medieval Rhetoric* (Indiana University Press, 1973).

5. Joseph Farrell in William Dominik, ed., *Roman Eloquence: Rhetoric in Society and Literature* (Routledge, 1997).

6. Rita Copeland, *Rhetoric, Hermeneutics and Translation in the Middle Ages* (Cambridge University Press, 1991) p. 161.

7. Edmond Faral (ed.), *Les Arts poétiques du 12me et du 13me siècle* (Champion, 1971).

8. Ibid., pp. 52-4.

9. *Poetria Nova*, trans. Margaret F. Nims (University of Toronto Press, 1967), p. 236.

10. [Cicero], *Ad Herennium*, trans. H. Caplan, Loeb Classical Library 403 (Harvard University Press, 1954), p. 375.

11. Quoted in Faral, op. cit., (above, n. 7), p. 358.

12. *Documentum de modo et arte dictandi et versificandi*, trans. Roger P. Parr (Marquette Press, 1968), p. 56.

13. Ibid., p. 55.

14. Ibid., pp. 56-7.

15. Augustine, *Confessions,* 6.3, trans. Henry Chadwick (Oxford University Press, 1992), p. 93.

16. Geoffrey of Vinsauf, *Documentum*, op. cit. (above, n. 11), pp. 56-7.

17. S. Johnson, *Everything Bad Is Good For You* (Riverhead, 2005), pp. 19-20.

18. E. Panofsky, ed. and trans., *Abbot Suger on the Abbey Church of Saint-Denis and its Art Treasures*, ed. G. Panofsky-Soergel (Princeton University Press, 1979), pp. 62-5.

19. *Oeuvres complètes de Suger*, ed. A. Lecoy de la Marche (Raynouard, 1867), *Chartes* 10, pp. 356-7.

20. Panofsky, op. cit. (above, n. 18), p. 87.

21. So, for example, the description given of Suger's accomplishments in his *Vita*: 'ex veteri novam, ex angusta latissimam, ex tenebrosiore splendidam redderent ecclesiam' ('which restored the new church from the old, the very wide from the narrow, the brilliant from the dark') (*Oeuvres*, op. cit., above, n.19, p. 391).

22. Rudyard Kipling, *Complete Verse: Definitive Edition* (Doubleday, 1940), pp. 87-8.

23. Text from Walter T. Pattison, *Life and Works of the Troubadour Raimbaut d'Orange* (University of Minnesota Press, 1954), pp. 121-3. Texts of other troubadour poems from *Anthology of the Provençal troubadours*, ed. T. Bergin, S. Olson, W. Paden, N. Smith (Yale University Press, 1973).

24. Joseph Anglade (ed.), *Les Origines du Gai Savoir* (Boccard, 1920); and A.F. Gatien-Arnoult (ed.), *Monumens de la littérature romane* (Bon et Privat, 1849).

25. Ibid., p. 360.

26. Ibid., p. 376.

27. Ibid., p. 376.

28. Daniel Heller-Roazen ties this to the interest in Neoplatonism in the twelfth century evidenced by the thinkers of the Chartrian school in their commentary on Plato's *Timaeus*. 'The Matter of Language: Guilhem de Peitieus and the Platonic Tradition', *MLN* 113 (1998), pp. 851-80.

4. The Chiastic Page: The Rhetoric of Montaigne's *Essais*

1. Vickers, op. cit., pp. 285-6. See also Marc Fumaroli, éd., *Histoire de la rhétorique dans l'Europe moderne, 1450-1950* (Presses Universitaires de France, 1999).

2. John Hollander, *Melodious Guile* (Yale University Press, 1988), pp. 118, 127, 129.

3. Anne Bradstreet, *Letter to Her Son*, in *The Complete Works of Anne Bradstreet*, ed. Joseph R. McElrath, Jr. and Allan P. Robb (Twayne, 1981), p. 195.

4. Thomas Wilson, *The Art of Rhetoric*, ed. P. Medina (Penn State Press, 1994).

5. Henry Peacham, *The Garden of Eloquence* (Scolar Press, 1971).

6. Mosellanus (Petrus Schade), *Tabulae de schematibus et tropis* (Cologne, 1526).

7. George Puttenham, *The Arte of English Poesie*, ed. G.D. Wilcock and A.

Walker (Cambridge University Press, 1970): 'Of Ornament', ch. 1, p. 138.

8. Thomas Greene, *The Vulnerable Text* (Columbia University Press, 1986), p. 17.

9. *Dictionnaire de Michel de Montaigne*, ed. Philippe Desan (Champion, 2004), pp. 874-6.

10. The text of the *Essais* quoted in this chapter is from *Les Essais de Michel de Montaigne*, ed. Pierre Villey (Presses Universitaires de France, 1965); the translation quoted is that of Donald Frame: Michel de Montaigne, *The Complete Works*, Everyman's Library 259 (Knopf, 2003), with minor changes. References in the text are to these volumes.

11. David Quint, *Montaigne and the Quality of Mercy: Ethical and Political Themes in the Essais* (Princeton University Press, 1998), p. ix.

12. Numbers in parentheses in this and the following paragraph refer to page numbers of Villey (above, n. 10).

13. *Montaigne's Annotated Copy of Lucretius*, ed. M.A. Screech (Droz, 1998).

14. Jacques Derrida, *Glas* (Galilee, 1974).

15. Terence Hawkes, *Shakespeare in the Present* (Routledge, 2002), p. 31.

16. *Montaigne's Lucretius* (above, n. 12), p. xx.

17. E.R. Curtius, *European Literature and the Latin Middle Ages*, trans. Willard R. Trask (Pantheon, 1953), pp. 487-94.

Conclusion

1. David Orr, 'Who Needs Mace? Whip Out That Sonnet', *New York Times Book Review*, 26 June 2005.

2. Wole Soyinka, 'Rhetoric that Binds and Blinds', *Climate of Fear: The Quest for Dignity in a Dehumanized World* (Random House, 2005), pp. 77, 82.

Select Bibliography

Akehurst, F.R.P. and Judith Davis (eds), *A Handbook of the Troubadours* (University of California Press, 1995).

Anglade, Joseph (ed.), *Les Origines du Gai Savoir* (Boccard, 1920).

Aristotle, *On Rhetoric: A Theory of Civic Discourse*, trans. George A. Kennedy (Oxford University Press, 1991).

Arnaut Daniel, *Poetry*, ed. James J. Wilhelm (Garland, 1981).

Augustine, *Confessions*, trans. Henry Chadwick (Oxford University Press, 1991).

Baldwin, Charles Sears, *Ancient Rhetoric and Poetic* (Peter Smith, 1959 [orig. pub. Macmillan, 1924]).

Barthes, Roland, 'The Old Rhetoric: An Aide-Mémoire', *The Semiotic Challenge*, trans. Richard Howard (Hill & Wang, 1988 [orig. pub. as 'L'Ancienne Rhétorique: Aide-mémoire' in *Communications* 16 (1970): 172-229]).

Baudrillard, Jean, *The Vital Illusion*, Wellek Library Lectures (Columbia University Press, 2000).

Benardete, Seth, *Rhetoric of Morality and Philosophy* (University of Chicago Press, 1991).

Billy, Dominique, *L'espace lyrique méditerranéen au Moyen Age* (Toulouse, 2006).

Booth, Wayne, *The Rhetoric of Rhetoric* (Blackwell, 2004).

Bradstreet, Anne, *The Complete Works of Anne Bradstreet*, ed. Joseph R. McElrath, Jr. and Allan P. Robb (Twayne, 1981).

Cancik, H. and H. Schneider (eds), *Brill's New Pauly: Encyclopaedia of the Ancient World* (Brill, 2004).

Caplan, Harry, *Of Eloquence: Studies in Ancient and Mediaeval Rhetoric*, ed. A. King and H. North (Cornell University Press, 1970).

Cave, Terence, *The Cornucopian Text* (Oxford University Press, 1979).

Cheyfitz, Eric, *Poetics of Imperialism* (University of Pennsylvania Press, 1997).

[Cicero], *Ad Herennium*, trans. H. Caplan, Loeb Classical Library 403 (1954; repr. Harvard University Press, 2004).

Cicero, *De Inventione*, trans. H.M. Hubbell, Loeb Classical Library 386 (1949; repr. Harvard University Press, 1976).

Cicero, *De Oratore*, trans. E.W. Sutton and H. Rackam, Loeb Classical Library 348 (1942; repr. Harvard University Press, 1979).

Cicero, *De Re Publica*, trans. C.W. Keyes, Loeb Classical Library 213 (1928; repr. Harvard University Press, 1977).

Cicero, *The Verrine Orations*, trans. L.H.G. Greenwood, Loeb Classical Library 221-2 (1928; repr. Harvard University Press, 1978).

Clark, M.L. *Rhetoric at Rome*, rev. edn (Routledge, 1996).

Cochran, Terry, *Twilight of the Literary: Figures of Thought in the Age of Print* (Harvard University Press, 2001).

Cole, Thomas, *Origins of Rhetoric in Ancient Greece* (Johns Hopkins University Press, 1991).

Copeland, Rita, *Rhetoric, Hermeneutics and Translation in the Middle Ages* (Cambridge University Press, 1991).

Curtius, E.R., *European Literature and the Latin Middle Ages*, trans. Willard R. Trask (Pantheon Books, 1953).

Dawson, John David, *Christian Figural Reading and the Fashioning of Identity* (University of California Press, 2002).

De Bruyne, E., *Étude d'esthétique médiévale* (Slatkine Reprints, 1975 [orig. pub. 1946]).

Derrida, Jacques, *Glas* (Galilee, 1974).

Desan, Philippe (ed.), *Dictionnaire de Michel de Montaigne* (Champion, 2004).

Desbordes, Françoise, *La Rhétorique antique: l'art de persuader* (Hachette, 1996).

Dixon, Peter, *Rhetoric* (Methuen, 1974).

Douglas, Mary and David Hull, *How Classification Works* (Edinburgh University Press, 1992).

Dominik, W. (ed.), *Roman Eloquence: Rhetoric in Society and Literature* (Routledge, 1997).

Eco, Umberto, *The Mysterious Flame of Queen Loana*, trans. Geoffrey Brock (Harcourt, 2005).

Erasmus, Desiderius, *Copia*, trans. Betty Knott (University of Toronto Press, 1991).

Faral, E. (ed.), *Les Arts poétiques du 12me et du 13me siècle* (Champion, 1971 [orig. pub. 1924]).

Fish, Stanley, 'Postmodern Warfare: The Ignorance of Our Warrior Intellectuals', *Harper's*, July 2002, pp. 33-40.

Fumaroli, Marc (ed.), *Histoire de la rhétorique dans l'Europe moderne, 1450-1950* (Presses Universitaires de France, 1999).

Garver, Eugene, *Aristotle's Rhetoric: An Art of Character* (University of Chicago Press, 1994).

Gatien-Arnoult, A.F. (ed.), *Monumens de la littérature romane* (Bon et Privat, 1849).

Gaunt, Simon and Sarah Kay, *The Troubadours: An Introduction* (Cambridge University Press, 1999).

Genette, Girard, *Figures of Literary Discourse* (Columbia University Press, 1982).

Geoffrey of Vinsauf, *Documentum de modo et arte dictandi et versificandi*, trans. Roger P. Parr (Marquette Press, 1968).

Geoffrey of Vinsauf, *Poetria Nova*, trans. Margaret F. Nims (University of Toronto Press, 1967).

Gerson, Paula Lieber (ed.), *Abbot Suger and Saint-Denis* (Metropolitan Museum of Art, 1986).

Goodman, Allegra, 'Pembroke Previsited', *American Scholar* (2004), 142-5.

Green, Jeffrey, 'Montaigne's Critique of Cicero', *Journal of the History of Ideas* 36 (1975), 595-612.

Greene, Thomas, *The Vulnerable Text* (Columbia University Press, 1986).

Grimaldi, William, *Studies in the Philosophy of Aristotle's Rhetoric,* Hermes 25 (Wiesbaden, 1972).

Habinek, Thomas, *Ancient Rhetoric and Oratory* (Blackwell, 2005).

Hawkes, Terence, *Shakespeare in the Present* (Routledge, 2002).

Heller-Roazen, Daniel, 'The Matter of Language: Guilhem de Peitieus and the Platonic Tradition', *MLN* 113 (1998), 851-80.

Henry, A., *Métonymie et métaphore* (Palais des Académies, 1984).

Hill, R.T., T.G. Bergin, S. Olson, W. Paden, N. Smith (eds), *Anthology of the Provençal Troubadours* (Yale University Press, 1973).

Hinds, Stephen. *Allusion and Intertext* (Cambridge University Press, 1998).

Holcomb, Chris, '"The Crown of all our Study": Improvisation in Quintilian's *Institutio Oratoria*', *Renaissance Society Quarterly* 31 (2001), 53-72.

Hollander, John, *Melodious Guile* (Yale University Press, 1988).

Hollander, John, *Rhyme's Reason* (Yale University Press, 1989).

Innes, D., 'Cicero on Tropes', *Rhetorica* 6 (1998), 307-25.

Jensen, Frede, *Troubadour Lyric: A Bilingual Anthology* (Peter Lang, 1998).

Johnson, S., *Everything Bad Is Good For You* (Riverhead, 2005).

Kallendorf, Craig (ed.), *Landmark Essays on Rhetoric and Literature* (Hermagoras Press, 1999).

Kennedy, George, *New History of Classical Rhetoric* (Princeton University Press, 1994).

Kennedy, George, *Classical Rhetoric and its Christian and Secular Tradition from Ancient to Modern Times*, 2nd edn (University of North Carolina Press, 1999).

Kipling, Rudyard, *Complete Verse: Definitive Edition* (Doubleday, 1940).

Kraye, Jill (ed.), *Cambridge Companion to Renaissance Humanism* (Cambridge University Press, 1996).

Lafont, Robert, *Histoire et anthologie de la littérature occitane: l'âge classique* (Presses du Languedoc, 1997).

Lanham, Richard, *The Motives of Eloquence: Literary Rhetoric in the Renaissance* (Yale University Press, 1976).

Lanham, Richard, *A Handlist of Rhetorical Terms*, rev. ed. (University of California Press, 1991).

Lausberg, H., *Handbook of Literary Rhetoric: A Foundation for Literary Study*, trans. Matthew Bliss, Annemiek Jansen, David Orton (Brill, 1998).

Lecoy de la Marche, A. (ed.), *Oeuvres complètes de Suger* (Raynouard, 1867).

Lestringant, F. (ed.), *Rhétorique de Montaigne* (Champion, 1985).

Lombreglia, Ralph, 'Massive Acts of Duplication', *Literary Imagination* 2.3 (2000), 300-13.

McFarlane, I.D. and Ian Maclean (eds), *Montaigne: Essays in Memory of Richard Sayce* (Oxford, 1982).

McGowan, Margaret, *Montaigne's Deceits: The Art of Persuasion in the Essais* (Temple University Press, 1974).

McKeon, Richard, 'Rhetoric in the Middle Ages', *Speculum* 17 (1942), 1-32.

Malamud, Martha, 'Gnawing at the End of the Rope', *Ramus* 27 (1998), 95-126.

Manieri, A., *L'immagine poetica nella teoria degli antichi* (Pisa, 1998).

Masters, Jamie, *Poetry and Civil War in Lucan's* Bellum Civile (Cambridge University Press, 1992).

Miller, Joseph, Michael H. Prosser, and Thomas W. Benson, *Readings in Medieval Rhetoric* (Indiana University Press, 1973).

Miller, Paul Allen, *Subjecting Verses* (Princeton University Press, 2004).

Milone, L., *El Trobar 'Envers' de Raimbaut d'Aurenga* (Columna, 1998).

Montaigne, Michel de, *Complete Works*, trans. Donald A. Frame. Everyman's Library 259 (Knopf, 2003).

Montaigne, Michel de, *Les Essais de Michel de Montaigne*, ed. Pierre Villey. (Presses Universitaires de France, 1965).

Mosellanus (Petrus Schade), *Tabulae de schematibus et tropis* (Cologne, 1526).

Murphy, James J., *Rhetoric in the Middle Ages*, rev. edn (Arizona Center for Medieval and Renaissance Studies, 2001).

National Commission on Terrorist Attacks, *The 9/11 Commission Report: Final Report of the National Commission on Terrorist Attacks Upon the United States* (Norton, 2004).

O'Brien, J., M. Quainton and J. Supple (eds), *Montaigne et la rhétorique: actes du colloque* (Champion, 1995).

Olmsted, W., *Rhetoric: An Historical Introduction* (Blackwell, 2006).

Orr, David, 'Who Needs Mace? Whip Out That Sonnet', *New York Times Book Review*, 26 June 2005.

Paden, William D., *An Introduction to Old Occitan* (Modern Language Association, 1998).

Panofsky, E. (ed.), *Abbot Suger on the Abbey Church of Saint-Denis and its Art Treasures*, 2nd edn, ed. G. Panofsky-Soergel (Princeton University Press, 1979).

Pattison, Walter T., *Life and Works of the Troubadour Raimbaut d'Orange* (University of Minnesota Press, 1954).

Peacham, Henry, *The Garden of Eloquence* (Scolar Press, 1971).

Pernot, Laurent, *Rhetoric in Antiquity*, trans. W.E. Higgins (Cambridge University Press, 2005) [orig. *La Rhétorique dans l'antiquité* (Librairie générale française, 2000)].

Plato, *Phaedrus*, trans. H.N. Fowler, Loeb Classical Library 36 (1914; repr. Harvard University Press, 1982).

Plato, *Symposium*, trans. W.R.M. Lamb, Loeb Classical Library 166 (1925; repr. Harvard University Press, 1975).

Poulakos, T. (ed.), *Rethinking the History of Rhetoric* (Westview Press, 1993).

Putnam, Michael C.J., *Poetry of the* Aeneid (Harvard University Press, 1965).

Puttenham, George, *The Arte of English Poesie*, ed. G.D. Wilcock and A. Walker (Cambridge University Press, 1970).

Quint, David, *Epic and Empire* (Princeton University Press, 1993).

Quint, David, *Montaigne and the Quality of Mercy: Ethical and Political Themes in the* Essais (Princeton University Press, 1998).

Quintilian, *The Orator's Education*, ed. and trans. Donald A. Russell, Loeb Classical Library 124-7 (Harvard University Press, 2001).

Rebhorn, Wayne, *Renaissance Debates on Rhetoric* (Cornell University Press, 2000).

Rendall, Steven, *Distinguo: Reading Montaigne Differently* (Oxford University Press, 1992).

Ricoeur, Paul, *La Métaphore Vive* (Seuil, 1975).

Rimmon-Keanan, Shlomith, 'The Paradoxical Status of Repetition', *Poetics Today* 1 (1980), 151-9.

Rosenberg, S., M. Switten and G. LeVot (eds), *Songs of the Troubadours and Trouvères* (Routledge, 1997).

Roubaud, Jacques. *La Fleur inverse: essai sur l'art formel des troubadours* (Editions Ramsay, 1986).

Screech, M.A., *Montaigne and Melancholy: The Wisdom of the* Essays (Duckworth, 1983).

Screech, M.A., *Montaigne's Annotated Copy of Lucretius* (Droz, 1998).

Sharon-Zisser, Shirley, 'A Distinction no Longer of Use: Evolutionary Discourse and the Disappearance of the Trope/Figure Binarism', *Rhetorica* 11 (1993), 321-42.

Sharpling, G.P., 'Towards a Rhetoric of Experience: The Role of *Enargeia* in the Essays of Montaigne', *Rhetorica* 20 (2002), 123-92.

Sloane, Thomas O., *Encyclopedia of Ancient Rhetoric* (Oxford University Press, 2001).

Soyinka, Wole, 'Rhetoric that Binds and Blinds', *Climate of Fear: The Quest for Dignity in a Dehumanized World* (Random House, 2005), 61-88.

Spence, Sarah, *Rhetorics of Reason and Desire* (Cornell University Press, 1988).

Spence, Sarah, *Texts and the Self in the Twelfth Century* (Cambridge University Press, 1996).

Starobinski, Jean, *Montaigne in Motion*, trans. Arthur Goldhammer (University of Chicago Press, 1985).

Stein, Robert and Sandra Prior, *Readings in Mediaeval Culture* (University of Notre Dame Press, 2005).

Thornton, M.K. and R.L. Thornton, 'The Financial Crisis of A.D. 33: A Keynesian Depression?', *Journal of Economic History* 50 (1990), 658-61.

Tournon, André, *Montaigne: La Glose et l'Essai*, rev. ed. (Champion, 2000).

Vasaly, Ann, *Representations: Images of the World in Cicero's Orations* (University of California Press, 1993).

Vickers, Brian, *In Defence of Rhetoric* (Oxford University Press, 1988).

Villey, Pierre, *Les Sources et l'évolution des Essais de Montaigne* (Hachette, 1908).

Villey, Pierre (ed.), *Les Essais de Michel de Montaigne* (Presses Universitaires de France, 1965).

Vitruvius, *Ten Books on Architecture*, trans. Ingrid D. Rowland (Cambridge University Press, 1999).

Ward, John O., 'Quintilian and the rhetorical revolution of the Middle Ages', *Rhetorica* 13 (1995), 231-84.

Wilson, Thomas, *The Art of Rhetoric*, ed. P. Medina (Penn State Press, 1994).

Wiseman, T.P., *Remus: A Roman Myth* (Cambridge University Press, 1995).

Ziolkowski, Theodore, *Hesitant Heroes: Private Inhibition, Cultural Crisis* (Cornell University Press, 2004).

Index

Index